Action Bronson
F*ck It, I'll Start Tomorrow

remember I went out on my fire escape one time to smoke, and they called the cops on me. They would also bang with the broom up from below if I made any noise; and I would bang with the broom back. Then, like an hour later, they wouldn't say anything standing right next to me in the elevator. It's crazy what living in an apartment is like.

People don't understand what it used to be like—that if you wanted to meet up with somebody, there was no calling them. You didn't have a phone. You had to just have faith that that person would show up. You had to have the place you would just go to, and it had to be the same place. And anything new you knew about, you had to find out about it yourself, or hear about it from word of mouth, then go find it. Now your favorite restaurant, put one thing out about it, and it'll be like McDonald's by the end of the week.

Even working in my father's restaurant, that was kind of a crew, with the Mexican guys I worked with just fucking with me all day long—us fucking with each other.

My family had owned a restaurant for years and years and years, since I was six, and so I had grown up in a professional-kitchen type of atmosphere—like a blue-collar-people kind of kitchen. When I was really young and my mother was making the desserts, I would always go hang out there and fuck around with the Ecuadorian chef, Rigoberto. He was the first chef who made me want to be there, in the kitchen. Later on, I worked there with Carlos, the Mexican dishwasher who was originally from Veracruz,* and Jusaid,

* I remember every time we were at work and someone would sneeze, they would go, *Ay yi yi, sancho.* I would say, *What the fuck you talking about, this sancho?* They told me that when you sneeze, El Sancho goes through the window and fucks your wife—it's, like, this guy with a mustache and

who was from Puebla. I worked with them both almost every day for ten years, and they taught me a lot about cooking, and they taught me how to speak Spanish. They were ill—they loved talking crazy and loved acting crazy, and they would usually only tell me how to say bad things, like *puto*.

When I was still in high school and did JV football for a bit, I was also part of that kind of fucking crew—a team. We were the Bayside Commodores, orange and blue, and we practiced every day with Coach Gay, who was a six-foot-eight black dude, three hundred pounds. We were like fucking lions, just fucking bashing each other—like lions or rams or those elk with the horns, just smashing into each other. It was tremendous. Every day we would practice and lift weights and fuck around. We had to run these quarter-mile sprints, or eighth-of-a-mile sprints, all the time, and that shit was crazy. So I was physically in really good shape then. I was running a lot, I was doing a lot of work, lifting lots of weights, and football was my thing, until I quit school.

Everyone was also always joking on each other at football practice, just like in the back of the bus. It was, you know, nonstop breaking balls. Nonstop. You know what a rat tail is? It's a towel—you have to spin it, make almost a knot in it. Wet it, then keep it moist, so that when you flick it, it's heavy. You ever been hit by one of those, you know that shit hurts. You get hit in the wrong spot by something that snaps like that? It's a whip. It was a normal thing at football practice to hit

---

a cape. And then he sneaks away, and it all happens through the window. So you don't ever want to sneeze. Carlos also told me that he doesn't let a woman go down on him because he believes that she could kill him if she blows into his dick hole. As I said, Carlos is from Veracruz, which is like the land of all the witch doctors, and black and white magic, and mystical lands.

each other with a rat tail. I've seen guys' balls explode. Almost. I used to be legendary with the rat tail. I could develop it, wet it, fashion it into a whip carefully, perfectly. I would make welts on legs, on ass cheeks and on rib cages.

We fucking did all kinds of crazy shit at football camp, like make rat tails, or beat people with the soap in a sock. Hold people down and beat them with hockey sticks. I don't know why there was a hockey stick at football camp, but there was. It's a hazing—people just hold you down and beat you up real quick and that's it. Everyone gets it. They're not doing it to jump you, they're doing it to haze you. They hit you with things, like soap or a sack full of tennis balls—it hurts, but it does toughen you up.

I mean, I'm not a bully. And I'm not that type of guy anymore. I don't like making fun of people anymore or any of that kind of stuff, and I don't find it amusing anymore. That's just gym stuff, football team stuff. It's childhood shit, is what it is, and at that point in life no one is the coolest guy on the block, and everyone is a fucking asshole, you know what I mean?

But I didn't stop football camp for those reasons. I actually stopped doing football 'cause I didn't want to do the summer camp anymore. I don't know if you've heard of two-a-days: it means we would practice twice a day—once in the morning, once in the afternoon. You'd practice literally till you threw up, in the heat, in the summertime. And I just wanted to smoke weed with my friends and have sex with my girlfriend, to be honest with you.

I said, *I'm done with this shit*, and I fucking got on the train and left camp, and that was it both for camp and for school. I was done. I bounced.

The Toothbrush Incident

My mother always wanted me to do good in school, and all the other things that all parents want. And I love her, she is the best. But I never finished high school—I gave it up to go chase my dreams, which at that point was smoking weed every day. Maybe I'd meet up in front of the school to go smoke weed all day long, maybe I'd be around the school smoking weed. Sometimes we'd go in, sometimes not. To me, school didn't matter, and nobody was going to make me go.

I've always been uncontrollable. I've always just done what I wanted. A few of my favorite stories:

The night before the Jets home opener when Brett Favre was going to play for the first time. It was two in the morning, I stopped at the store a block up from my house. I went in there for a vanilla Dutch and a $10 Win for Life scratch-off, and I left the fucking keys in the car and the car running. Because it was my neighborhood and that's what I always did. I come out, there's no fucking car there. The two sixteen-year-old shmucks that were there in front of the store crashed it into somebody's house in Long Island and burned it. My mother wasn't that happy: it was her car, and it was totally my fault.

And I used to have to open my family's restaurant early for brunch, but I didn't have a key, so I had to climb through the window of the restaurant to get in every morning. One day this lady is jogging by as I'm breaking into the restaurant to go work, and she starts screaming at the top of her lungs that she's going to call the cops. I start cursing, a war of words ensues, a war of words. Later on Yelp she wrote like a massive paragraph about how she saw the chef breaking into the restaurant.

Or the time me and Body were at the Michael Jordan party at Cipriani's on Wall Street, so all the power athletes and everybody were there. Derek Jeter, Moses Malone, Nicki Minaj. Magic Johnson and Dominique Wilson and Clyde Drexler. And Prince, who performed in some secret corridor that you had to find. We were all having dinner, and everyone started screaming and running because Prince was performing in some secret corridor. We saw Prince for a minute, but then me and Body were just fucking blowing down a blunt in a dressing room with nobody around.

I always smoke weed freely, always have and always will: I don't care what other people say, or if the police stop me. I would always be the one who lit up in the street, and everyone would be like, *Oh, you're crazy.* I was always that guy, 100 percent. I'll just light the blunt anywhere. I've only not gotten away with it one time in high school, when I was smoking a blunt by Bayside High, a story I've told before. I got bagged up walking the back streets of Bayside: these detectives were set up in a Mercury Villager minivan with a baby seat, using tricks like they were trying to find a serial killer, but on two kids smoking weed. They did this at 9:00 a.m. and we had to sit around handcuffed in the van for six hours till they finished their shift, though they did uncuff one hand when they bought us McDonald's.

I mean, I've been arrested so many times—there's been fighting, there was once with weed, lots of driving with no license because I let it expire. But my ratio of times talking my way out of something to being arrested is pretty good. I say, *Listen, man, don't even run my ID.* You've just got to level with them sometimes. Don't make them do all the unnecessary dumb shit, because once they put it in the system and they find out you don't have a license, they have to take you in. Usually it's just a summons, and then I have to go to court. But if you talk to them prior, lay down the game that you don't have one, it'll often go your way. I've used the *I have to take a shit* excuse, or *My girl is pregnant. My mother's handicapped. My father's this*—I have run the gamut of all the excuses you can probably think of. Most of the time it is me saying I have to shit really bad, but then again, why am I in the car in the first place? It's happened at least fifteen times, and will happen again until they get sick of me and tell me I gotta go in for ninety days.

When we would get pulled over when we were younger, there was always some fucking hijinks that went on—trying to hide the weed, trying to hide whatever was in the car. I was a master at throwing it under my nuts. And I was also a master of working it in between my butt cheeks while driving. It's like doing a bicycle kick while you're driving. For smoking weed in the park, I used to not wear underwear just in case the cops came. The cops would always roll up in there, checking us up, patting us down, so I devised a plan to let them know that I wasn't wearing any underwear. We got caught in the park smoking weed one time, and they were going in everybody's little pockets. I was like, *Listen, I don't have pockets, I don't even have underwear on*. And it actually worked. I had weed under my nuts, like a bag of it; at the time it couldn't have been more than a couple grams, but it still saved me from going in for a night. So that was a small victory. You know, you have to take small victories and turn them into larger victories.

After that I stopped wearing underwear to the park at all—I would just be wearing basketball shorts, like St. John's practice shorts, very thin. I'd go home, take off the underwear, save them for when I got back home to put them on again and chill, then go to the park in just the shorts. First off, I just thought it was funny, and I figured they would never want to touch me if I really wasn't wearing underwear.

To be honest, this really started because the cops, they always used to ask to smell your hand for weed—you know, *Lemme smell your hand.* So before I went to the park I would just dig under my nuts, deeply. I mean, I had just been playing ball and whatever, so it was definitely bad company down there, it was bad business. It's *Big Trouble in Little China* down there, you know what I am saying? This cop asked to smell my fingers, and he caught a whiff of some fucking wang. He caught a big whiff of the wang,* and he was disgusted, and it made me happy.

So maybe I have a long history of questionable behavior. I mean, I have humility also—I was always good to my mother and my grandparents. I would help the little old ladies across the street, they all knew me as a nice boy. Which was crazy because, you know, that's the real me also. The real me is also that nice boy.

---

* It is what it is. The thing is, everyone has some sort of stench somewhere, if you get deep into smelling somebody. If I fucking get up and walk across the room, it stinks. If I just get out of the shower, it stinks. Even though I've always washed well. You always have to wash well. Once you start getting interested in the opposite sex or the same sex or whatever have you, you want to start washing, because there's the potential that someone else might smell down there. And you don't want to turn them off, or you at least don't want them to tell anyone. Maybe it doesn't matter if it turns them off, but only as long as they don't tell anyone.

But look at any picture of me from growing up and you can tell. That boy always did what he wanted.

I remember one time, when I was maybe ten, when I used to walk around in the street playing rap music out of my radio that had a tape deck and one speaker. One of the guys in the neighborhood, he was like a southern guy, and he told me to turn my music down, he was hating on me, and I called him a redneck motherfucker. He went and told my grandmother—my nonna—and she came down and she slapped me, I think the only time she ever did that. She had no clue what *redneck* even meant, what I had said to him, she just knew I was doing something wrong.

Even when I was in elementary school, I used to yell and scream a lot and act up, cursing and talking crazy. I remember my mom taking me to see two psychologists. The first one, this Jewish guy, I remember being very combative, like, *I don't want to go to this fucking asshole.* I went into the room with him, played games, like Clue and tic-tac-toe and Connect Four, and he gave me rugelach, and that's all I remember. I don't remember getting anything done, I don't remember any fucking emotional breakthroughs. But the rugelach, which is a Jewish pastry, that's what I remember from therapy.

The second psychologist was at Queens College, right near my neighborhood. It was people preparing to be therapists—you know, like when they send you to the dentist and they actually let the students do it? That's what this was. So the lady, on my application there, asked me if I played with shit: *Do you play with your or anyone else's feces?* Because that's the sign of a sicko. I mean, there's so many other signs, but that one's a crazy one. I said no, but in retrospect, there's been two times, perhaps three times. Okay, maybe there were four times, now that I think on it. Let's say three times, with one having a part A and a part B.

The first time I played with shit—it just sounds crazy, right?—was when I was maybe sixteen. I put shit on the handle of the door at the mall bathroom, just to fuck with somebody. It could have been anyone. It wasn't actual shit— it was just a piece of toilet paper and I rubbed it in the shit. I had dignity. You want to know how I got out of the bathroom myself without touching the handle? I used the door stopper. So this was totally premeditated. This was a long, long time ago—I was a shithead. I've also done that at a Subway restaurant.

There is also the toothbrush incident.* And this is something I have never told anyone. I might not tell you now. There's a picture of me and some friends from this period of my life where I have a chin strap and a sprained leg and I am holding up a Woodchuck cider—that's all I am going to say. Let's leave this one alone—it's over.

And then there was a fecal moment at fat camp, where there was this kid I didn't like, that I fought with and gave several kicks to the groin of. There was a log of shit in the toilet, and I just took his shoe and scooped out the log of shit with it and then put the shoe on a swing. I didn't even

* This is one reason why I don't like to use the same toothbrush more than twice, really. They're nasty once you have them for too long, all that stuff that you're brushing isn't just going away from the brush with water. Still hasn't helped me, though; I need to get my shit whitened. All I do is smoke weed and drink Snapple—I am on like the fucking fifth scale away from white.

have to touch the shit. I should have just left the shoe for him to slide his foot into in his room, but instead I left it on display, like when you leave the king's head after you cut it off in the guillotine.

I got kicked out of camp for that. After I confessed—and after someone snitched.

My mom had to come get me. Anything I've ever gone away to, my mother had to come get me at. She wasn't pissed, because my mother is my ride or die, and she's also a free spirit herself. She laughs at the things I do. If I put shit on a swing, she's laughing at it. It was also close to the end of camp, which was six weeks long, so really, when you think about it, I just got an early release for bad behavior.

That was my second year at that camp, and I was like the wildest person there, people just couldn't understand me. Mad crazy shit happened at camp because of me—I mean it was six weeks long, who wouldn't do crazy things. But I made it work, I had some friend-type people, and I also moved some fucking weight.

Listen, I don't want to set up fat camp as a real sad scene; it wasn't like a total fat farm. It was more like Judd Apatow's movie *Heavyweights*, at an upstate place called Camp Shane. Apatow was born in Flushing, too, and he even went up to that camp to check it out for the movie, which I know because I asked him.

Of course, people called it Camp Shame because it was for fat people, and I did get picked up in a miserable parking lot and went on a miserable bus ride to camp. I still remember having a lot of rap CDs with me and mad *Source* magazines to read on the ride. I had a subscription, and later on in the summer my mother would mail the latest issues to me at camp—I remember the Puff Daddy and the Family issue came out while I was there. I also had subscriptions to *GamePro, Vibe, Sports Illustrated, Sports Illustrated Kids*, and *Highlights.* Mom sent me all those, and a lot of other shit—letters and CDs. And of course she saved all the fucking letters I would write to her: *Yo, mom, come save me, I hate this fucking place.* She saved all of them—it's like forty postcards. It's going to be an art exhibit one day.

But really, camp wasn't that bad, and it wasn't embarrassing to me. I've fluctuated in weight my entire life, but no matter what, I am a fairly good athletic person—I am better at doing most athletic things than even a regular person. So think about that: I was definitely the athletic standout at Camp Shame.

Most people there weren't crazy fat—there were regular people, too, people who just wanted to be healthier, people who had already lost weight and wanted to keep it off. The majority of kids were not that big, they were just overweight in their parents' eyes, or in society's eyes, people whose parents considered slightly chubby as being fat, and the parents wanted to fucking nip it in the bud because we're all twelve, thirteen years old, you know what I mean? They wanted to prevent future hangage and make it so you weren't sitting around all summer fucking eating shitty food all day long, but so you were exercising and eating right instead.

But there were some fat motherfuckers, you know? There's no doubt, there were definitely some behemoths.

When your knees in the back are so fat you don't have a shape to your calf, and your shoes are so tight that the tongue points forward? And you can only wear, like, hospital shorts. Even at Camp Shame you would get made fun of for that, unfortunately. It's kind of a sad situation, isn't it? When you're fat, if someone's fatter than you, even a little bit, then you feel better about yourself. It's kind of ridiculous. But hopefully those people got help. Most people were there to move some fucking weight, and a lot of people did.

To be honest, it was fun. It was all the things you do in a normal camp, you just get terrible turkey meat on whole wheat bread for lunch, or popcorn for a snack, or whole wheat toast with apple butter for breakfast—every morning we had apple butter. But we still drove go-karts. We still ran the track. Motherfuckers playing video games in the video game room. I would lift weights, play basketball, tennis, hockey. I also remember there was always one "family day" when my mother would come through. One summer she brought me a pair of fucking crazy Nike Air Maxes and took me for Chinese food up there in the mall.

There were also those times when they let you out at night so you could mingle with the girls, and most of these girls were not fat at all. There were several that were in really good shape. By that age—junior high school—you're not fully confident in that situation yet. Someone kisses you, your fucking dick gets hard. Someone looks at you, your dick gets hard. *Here we go.* You know, *Now we're off to the races.* One girl asked to see my penis and I had jogging pants on, and I had to fluff it for a second. I didn't want to show it just like that, so I just fluffed it, and then I showed it to her. It all happened quickly because, of course, it got me hard when she asked me.

I remember you would have to walk to the outskirts and go over this fence and lay in the grass. That's where I got my dick sucked—this was a secret area that I found, where you could go out into the woods behind the bunks in the women's area.*

I mean, you know me, you know I'm not following any of the rules, ever. I'm doing what I want, even at fat camp. I got cool with the counselors, so I would be chilling with them. I didn't have to do the activities, the set of things we were supposed to do. I could just run the track if I wanted or just do go-karts all day. I would go to the weight room, just working out with the fucking dude that was the counselor for the whole camp, hanging at the gym all day.

I even used to sneak Big Macs into my bunk. One of the counselors used to get me anything I wanted. She would bring me the stuff and I would sell it off: Big Macs, chicken sandwiches, burgers, McNuggets, a bucket of fried chicken, whatever. She one million percent helped me with the illicit Snickers and the peanut butter M&M's. She smuggled both for my personal use as well as for sale—in the middle of the night sometimes. She would fucking bring me in a fucking Big Mac and McNuggets, and I'd be in there at midnight in

* All my early sex moves were from porn, from reggae videos or movies, or just switching back and forth between channels 62 and 63 on cable, because there was a pause in the cable where you would see like a tit, or you could see a piece of ass. And seeing all kinds of crazy shit in magazines that you steal from the store, laughing at the word *dick*. I think I've come a long way from laughing at the word *dick*. Yet I still laugh at the word *dick*—think about it. You're an asshole if you don't.

the bunk eating, while everyone's going nuts. And of course, I'd have to wet everyone's beak. There were definitely kids there that lost no weight because they were just eating those burgers. I stuck to it, though, I actually lost about thirty or forty pounds.

I remember coming into high school after that summer, after I lost all that weight at camp, working out. I wore a fucking pair of Avirex jeans with an urban knitted sweater, tucked in. I tucked it the fuck in, into some fucking baggy-ass jeans, and wore it with Timboos. I looked crazy—it was a wild look, it was heavy-duty. Maybe my fashion game wasn't totally on par at that point, but I was on fire—that was the look. I'm sure I was killing it. I was killing the game, because I was coming up with something different. You know, I was flipping the script on 'em.

That summer I had lost my virginity to that same counselor that smuggled me the McDonald's. She came into the bunk, and there were fourteen other kids in there and she took me right there. She had nerve, right? I told her I was seventeen, but I was thirteen or fourteen. I was obviously not seventeen years old. Everyone was sleeping, and she was riding my fourteen-year-old dick, and I came in literally five seconds. Well, I'm giving myself that. It was more like two seconds. One pump, and I was ready to go. Then I tried to fake-eat her pussy. I was down there and I was like, *What is this?* So I just said, *I came.* And that was that.

She broke all kinds of rules. She broke the ethics of life. Abusing her position of power, endangering the welfare of the children. It may have even traumatized some people in the room—maybe now they can only have sex in groups. I don't even remember how it all went down, but

I do remember telling her I had a ten-inch cock, when in fact I did not have a ten-inch cock. I was walking around like I knew how to fuck. Ridiculous. I mean, looking back, it was just pretty amazing that I told her that, and that she believed that I did. Then we were kissing, and she was like, *Well, what happened?*

I Come from a Rebel Family

Another one of the reasons I am where I am today is because my mother is a New York original, a classic weirdo New York Jew, originally from Brownsville, Brooklyn. She was born at St. Marks Avenue and Saratoga, like the same place as M.O.P. is from, but when Brownsville was full of immigrant Jews just off the boat from Ellis Island and the phone exchange was still Dickens 2 something-something. When my mother's family lived there, you'd have to pick up the phone and say that to somebody to get to her. My grandfather moved them to Queens when my mom was about eleven, to the same two-bedroom apartment in Electchester that I grew up in. My mother's lived there almost her whole life.

My mother never ever cared what people thought, exactly. She gave no fucks. My mom did all kinds of weird shit, and still does. She had a whole life until she had me—she was already forty, and then she had me. She almost died because she lost so much blood, and so she couldn't have any other children. Up until then, my mother was in the Manhattan music and art scene, like downtown and bookstores and shit like that, and she still does amazing paintings. She actually met my father because they were both musicians, they did gigs together. But my parents got divorced when I was in junior high school, and ever since then, it was just us.

Having a mom that was a rebel and a free spirit and took LSD and smoked weed and shit like that was a fucking plus, somebody who understood me, who always supported me. I have a pretty fucking good mom, and good moms help in life, no doubt about that. She was the one who really taught me that if you don't look like everyone else, you just have to not give a shit, to love yourself even more.

But she was cool beyond that—she used to always let

the kids smoke weed in the house, me and my friends, so we wouldn't get in trouble. I came home one day stoned out of my mind, and she said, *Ariyan, you fucking stoned out of your mind?* When I said yes, she was like, *Cool. You can smoke here, if you want.*

My mom let us smoke in the house because she wanted us to be safe, but also because she really likes weed. She'd knock on the door when I was smoking with my friends and she'd just make a little movement with her eyes. We'd know what that meant: she'd come in and take a little hit and then leave.

We used to go to the mall a lot together, too. In Florida, where my American grandparents lived, and all over the city— because at the mall, you have all kinds of things to do together: The food court. The good sports store, where I would always like to roam around for hours. The music store—maybe Sam Goody, or Coconuts. We'd hit the Queens Center mall, we'd drive to Old Country Road in Long Island, right there next to the Sports Authority complex. I admit that type of shit used to excite me, just the possibilities in those stores. We would go see movies together—my mom took me to see *New Jack City*, she took me to *Juice* and *Boyz n the Hood*, all at the theater where there were fucking shootings, and people always screaming at the movie. There was a shooting for everything there—there was a fucking shooting for *Mrs. Doubtfire*.

My mother and I would also go explore the Costco on Old Country Road, when it was still called Price Club. One of my favorite memories from there is how I would wander off and taste all the samples, and when my mother couldn't find me, she would jingle the keys on this silver key chain she had. One of my other favorite memories with my mother is in the summers: when my Albanian cousins and I were home from school and we weren't at some day camp,* we all went to Robert Moses State Park, or if we could get there early enough to find parking, Jones Beach Field 6 in the Rockaway state park in Queens—it had the shortest walk from the car. We'd hit the bagel store near our house on the way there and order a couple of sandwiches, and later we would eat them, still dripping wet, sitting in the shade under the umbrella on a blanket with my mother.

We also explored restaurants all over the city. I did it with my mother before I ever did it with my friends. My mother had a friend named Helen who used to own the Chinese restaurant across the street from my house with her husband, Joe. Me and my mother and Helen and Helen's Korean friend Theresa and her son, who was my age, we all became good friends. And they would always take us out to eat at the good places in Chinatown and along Main Street in the Queens Chinatown.

Growing up my mother was always going places, always taking me places, cooking with me and for me. She was the best, she exposed me to so much shit just being a free spirit herself. My road dog, my road warrior—you know, I feel like there's no doubt about it that my mom gave me spirituality and the love of just going around the city.

---

* When I didn't go to the beach I would play at this ill day camp on Roosevelt Island. We all went to day camp in the summer—in the fucking city, man, parents want to get rid of you during the day, you're not going to be in your fucking small apartment all day. You play basketball and handball and they take you swimming in different city pools and shit like that— but I don't really like pools. That's the one place I don't swim. I don't like chlorine, and one of my fucking pet peeves is stepping on a city pool floor, because I've seen the logs of shit before at a city pool, I'm dead-ass.

I also gained a lot of knowledge hanging out with my mother's father, my American grandfather, whose name was Irving Lovett. He gave me incredible knowledge about every-thing—to love good food and eating out, to have a huge love for boxing and wrestling and watching tons of movies,* with how to be funny around people and how to just live life. He came to the United States on a boat to Ellis Island, and he spoke Yiddish and English with one of those old-timey New York accents. He was a big guy with a beautiful head of white hair and he was funny in a very Rodney Dangerfield–esque way. That's how I got to be funny, too, watching him. He was a fucking riot. He would have the whole room going—at restaurants, at the airport.

By the time I came along, my American grandpar-ents had already moved out of the apartment and retired to Florida, to West Palm Beach, where a bunch of their friends had also moved. My grandmother was in a nursing home, she had Alzheimer's as long as I could remember her, but my grandfather loved to take us to restaurants. Our day started with breakfast together at the bagel shop, and in Florida the bagel shops weren't the little deli-like things they are in New

* We still have stupid amounts of my grandfather's VHS movies at my mother's house. Those got sent up from Florida after he died—that's my inheritance. He loved movies, that was his thing. There's great stuff in there, but also things like *Oklahoma!*, *Fiddler on the Roof*, *South Pacific*—I wasn't watching that shit. Now I can't even watch them because I don't have a VCR. I still have all my old DVDs, too. I would love to have them all digitalized. Renting movies on tape was a big thing for me growing up. Going to Blockbuster taught you responsibility—you had to turn them in on time or else you got a fee, and no one wants to get a fee. And you wanted to take it back to get a new one—the trick was to look in the return because, the newest movie or game out, they only allowed you to rent it for one day. I used to rent some weird shit from Blockbuster—I remember renting Dreamcast, I don't know why, that shit was wack.

York City, they're more like diners. He would have the waitresses eating out of the palm of his hand, and then they'd walk away and he'd talk shit about them. He was fucking hilarious. Later on he was in a wheelchair, he'd be rowing the wheelchair like a boat, making everyone laugh. Those trips out to eat were always a highlight for the three of us, and now they're still a highlight for me and my mom.

I actually have rebel family on both sides. My Albanian grandparents—Arslan and Alije, who I always called Nonna—were originally from Kosovo, but then they fled when things got bad in Communist Yugoslavia. My grandparents were on their way to Turkey and made it to Macedonia, to a city called Skopje, and ended up staying there. One of my uncles came to America first, my father came next, then everybody else came after that.

When you make it from a communist country in turmoil from afar just to make it to freedom? That's a rebel. Obviously, you've got to respect those people, because they fucking came from nothing and went for it, and they made it. Some of my Albanian uncles started out painting buildings, and then they fucking bought a building, back when you could still buy a building in New York.

A lot of New York City building supers are Albanian—they get each other jobs being a super. It's like a network. It's a prestigious job, and you get a free apartment. My uncle was the fucking super in the building where Christopher Walken grew up on Thirty-First in Astoria. He had a massive apartment, with the building rec room right next to it, and no one was ever in it. My cousin had her sweet sixteen there. We used to play drums in there, all kinds of ping-pong for free.

They had a stickball thing, so we used to hit the stickball. You would have to call him at the bar if you needed your plumbing fixed or something. There were no cell phones back then, so you would have to call him over at Kelly's, and then he would go right back to the bar after he was done. One hundred percent.*

My Albanian grandparents slept on the couch in our living room until my parents split up when I was about twelve, six of us in a small two-bedroom apartment. Sometimes my Albanian uncles and my aunts, and their kids—I grew up with a lot of cousins—stayed at our house, too. When all my family came over in the eighties and nineties, they just immigrated to one house. Our apartment was a safe haven for Albanian refugees. There were no cell phones or emails, they just showed up. They would just get the address from another relative and just come.

Cigarettes everywhere, someone was usually sleeping at all times. I learned how to not make noise and to chill out during the day because my Albanian grandfather liked to take naps. Actually, the apartment wasn't that small, it just had a

---

* Albanian people, in New York, could be a super, they could work in a pizzeria, or they could work as a doorman. Or maybe a wedding singer. Those are the four main jobs, for men. Being a wedding singer's a big deal back home, because there are a lot of Albanian weddings and the singer's the crown jewel. Being a wedding singer is a big job over there—you can be very famous, if you're good, and you'll live well; though, no one's exactly fucking Dean Martin over there. It's usually a man—you know, there's no women allowed on the men's side in a Muslim wedding, but they do allow a woman singer. When I was at my cousin's wedding in Macedonia when I was seventeen—the same time the blackout happened in New York City— people were screaming, shooting guns in the air, making all kinds of whistles at the singer. Mainly I am just setting this as the scene where the wedding is actually separated. Men and women, they don't see each other until they finally do the marriage part, in the mosque, where it's very subdued.

lot of people and a lot of stuff in it, every surface covered with lace doilies my grandmother would make, and throw rugs. Somebody once told me you know you're an immigrant if you had a woven blanket with a tiger on it. We had the tiger one, we had the eagle one, we had all kinds of ones. We'd always sit in the living room, me on the floor, and watch TV together— it's how they learned to speak English, from the commercials. My grandmother would say, *Where's the beef?* And my grandfather would do the *Time to make the donuts* thing.

Albanians also like to visit each other's houses. Even here, they like to visit with each other, so there would be ten, twenty people sitting all night in our house, and you'd drink tea all night or drink fucking ouzo or raki and there would always be a lot of food. They'd just talk about nothing, just fucking bullshit, always with a pile of slippers inside the house, right at the door.* When we would go to Albanian parties at my great-aunt's house in Brooklyn, a lot of people in the family were musicians, so they would get together to play music, and everyone would cook together, my grandmother and my aunts. There's a lot of music and food in my family—we all

---

* There's always a pile of slippers inside the house, right at the door. So once again you put on whoever's shoes are there to take the garbage out, which is the illustrated story of me having to run from the fucking bear in the Poconos with my aunt's shoes in my first cookbook, *Fuck, That's Delicious.* You put on the ones that are easiest to put on and then you go. So sometimes slippers are unavailable; you know, they're like a Blockbuster movie. They get rented out, or sometimes they'll be left somewhere else, like in the fucking return box. We went there twice for family vacations, it was a trailer park called Eagle Lake. We had two trailers, and I guess this was like 1993 or so, because I remember my older cousin, a boy, and he had just gotten the white Reebok Pump Shaqs and he went to go play basketball at the Poconos basketball court. It was in this developed trailer park, a summer getaway for people who were from the city but didn't have a lot of money. I had a great time—and the Poconos don't ever get like the Hudson Valley because they're still a little scummy.

saw each other at the restaurant in Forest Hills, my grand-father was even a waiter, before he came to New York.

One of my uncles, Uncle Muzi, he married an Italian woman from Calabria. Early on, for Thanksgiving, we would all go over to their house in Brooklyn, and her father, who didn't speak any English, would make this ill Italian feast, oh my god, like meatballs and the rigatoni with eggplant, which was his favorite. That was one of the best parts of going to my Albanian family's gatherings—a Thanksgiving where you get to eat all types of crazy Italian and Albanian food *and* watch football. It was a crazy mash-up—my mother would bring the coffee cake, of course, because she has always been a baker, and it's the fucking best coffee cake* I've ever had in my life.

When I think about those cousins, I think about watching *The Twilight Zone* and having peppers and eggs with that Italian sliced white bread that always has the Italian flag on the side of the bag—that's what we always had there, sitting in the kitchen. My other cousins, the ones who used to live in Astoria and were a little older than me, they used to spoil me like a little bastard, take me ice-skating, and I would learn from them about clothes and sneakers and music.

---

* As I have said many times before, my mother's coffee cake, peach pie, and her most famous creation, the chocolate raspberry layer cake, are the three dishes I have seen the most in my life. She used to make the desserts for our family's restaurant, and wedding cakes, too. She's also always made an amazing lemon meringue pie. Oh man, her lemon meringue pie, for some reason, like it's extra heavy-duty. It always tastes like a marshmallow, with this extra thick and tall fluff. She used to do it amazingly. And she used to make a fucking tiramisu that was to die for, literally. I don't even like coffee, but I like it with sugar and milk, or in ice cream and desserts. I don't ever order it, but I do taste it. You know? It doesn't fucking nauseate me. Certain coffees that I've tasted early on nauseated me, probably because it wasn't a good quality coffee. Like Folgers, those little grounds of pencil shavings. Who even knew coffee was a bean back in the day? I just thought it came in a goddamn can.

Childhood is fun when you always have cousins around—I always did shit with them. It was fucking amazing. It was a beautiful, great childhood. That doesn't happen as much anymore; I don't think anyone even talks to each other—it always happens like that, with every culture, every family, and it's always over some stupid shit, too.

One thing about Albanians, they like to smoke—they smoke more than they eat, and they like to eat. My Albanian family used to bake out my mother's house with cigarettes, all different kinds of cigarettes. Everyone smoked a different brand: There was Marlboro Red. There was Marlboro Lights, and Rothmans Blue, an expensive English cigarette. And then when the cousins and aunts came over, one aunt smoked the Kent soft pack, it was beige, burgundy, and gold, with the long ones, the 100s, the slims, and she pounded them. Ten, twenty people in the house, everyone is talking heavy-duty and smoking nonstop—and with carpeting. There was this circular smoke disk on the ceiling for years in that apartment, we had to fucking detox when everyone left.

Being from an Albanian family, I've been forced to smoke, even though I don't smoke. When I went to Macedonia for the first time, after my grandfather died and my grandmother moved back, they take you around to people's houses and they offer you things. They think you smoke, so they give you a cigarette and, apparently, you can't say no, or else it's disrespectful.* You have to smoke the cigarette and

* Albanians also always fight over a bill at a restaurant, knowing neither of you want to pay it. I don't think anyone ever splits it. You fight to the death. It's literally the fucking staring game. Who's going to blink first? It's like a poker match—who's gonna fold? You win if you don't pay, but either way you lose because if you don't pay, the other person has power over you.

eat the stuffed pepper, even if the stuffed pepper is not from someone who makes it as good as your grandmother. I don't want this stuffed pepper when I've had my grandmother's stuffed pepper, you know what I mean?

Recently I went out to dinner on Christmas Eve with Dua Lipa and her family, and they're all Albanian, and we went to a steak house somewhere in Midtown owned by Albanians. It was a regular steak house, with regular steak house shit, but then the guy that owned it went to his mother's house and got the peppers and brought her peppers to the table. It was fucking crazy.

This is actually how I know how good of a cook my grandmother was, because as an Albanian you always end up tasting other people's home food, and she was by far in the top fucking echelon of chef. The way she prepped it, the way she made it, and how good it looked. She would get upset at herself if it had too much something or not enough, she would get mad every time, even if it was perfect. She would be happy with it one day, then not the next. Sometimes the bread would rise slowly, sometimes it would work too good and spill over. Even back then, I knew that the weather changed the day, the way it came out. She would usually say something negative, but then every once in a while, she would be like, *Ah. This is good. This is good pite.* It was a practice, you know, a work ethic. You work at what you were made to do. It took me a long time to get to that same spot in my own life, but I see it now.

I have a photograph of my grandmother rolling out these little square pouches filled with meat: she has the wooden dowel I now have, she is working on a *tepsia*, a big round metal pan flipped upside down so she can use it to roll the dough. I can still picture her cutting vegetables, cutting the tomatoes and the long green peppers right into the pot, holding the knife right against her thumb. That thumb was just so hard—you couldn't cut that thumb.

I always make my grandmother's stew with eggs, tomato, and red and green peppers. It's like shakshuka, just tomatoes and red peppers cooked down, like fried down really well. And then you just add eggs and cook them into a soft scramble. That's awesome: she called it *sugliash*; the Turks call it *menemen*.

My grandmother was an incredible cook, baker, everything. Constantly making food, three meals a day, every day. She always had all these things prepared in the fridge, you just go and nosh. I remember waking up to the smell of fresh bread, always. My grandmother taught my mom, and my mom, who is also an incredible cook, taught my grandmother how to make brisket and shit like that. There was a lot of cooking, a lot of shopping for cooking, a lot of cleaning up after cooking. It was hard coming up trying to be a culinary artist, as the women in my family don't let the men touch anything. But even so, they rubbed off on me.

My grandmother took care of all of us. She did all this willingly and lovingly. It was not forced. But it's also just the way they were brought up in Communist Yugoslavia. A woman takes care of that. I don't think that many women have jobs in those small villages where my family lives even now, to be honest with you. There just aren't that many jobs, and every woman that you meet is at home. It's different now, but there are still those traditions.

My grandmother was tough, she didn't take any shit from my grandfather when I knew her. But at that point when an Albanian man married a woman, no matter what, she was supposed to become whatever he wants her to be, and he controls the situation. There's definitely arranged marriages still in Macedonia. But when you marry an American and you marry a woman like my mother, it's not going to happen like that. When my parents were still married, my father was dead serious about me being Muslim, and my mother would always fucking sneak in, like, fucking Jew and weirdo shit because she's a New York Jew and a weirdo. You already knew my mother's not going to fucking do what anybody says. Like I said, that's why I'm where I'm at right now, because my mother was a rebel.

I've been thinking a lot recently about confidence, and the things that enabled me to be who I am, and one of them is my mother, and one of them is also just knowing all the hardships both of my grandparents had to go through over there and to get here to America, and everything that came before me.

My father's side—they lived through terrible shit in the Balkans and moved here at the beginning of the Yugoslav Wars. My mother's side, they came through Ellis Island. My grandfather, an Eastern European Jew, fled from Europe and ended up in Queens, and then retired in Florida. The American Jewish dream. Before that he was a plumber—he worked as a plumber on the Alaskan pipeline; my mom even has pictures of him in a field with a grizzly bear.

And now when I look around, all my family is good— for them to be where they are, for me to be where I am? To actually be somebody in a place like New York City? That's huge. I feel like it was that struggle, the struggle to flee on both sides, the success now, that gave me so much insight.

With all that behind me—I'm good.

The Steroid Years

The best shape I've ever gotten into was a period we'll call the Steroid Years, about fifteen years ago. These years weren't about losing weight, they were about lifting heavy weights and fucking really training. Training for what, I don't know, but I was training. It was great: I was biking everywhere, constantly getting exercise. Then, during work at my father's restaurant, I'd be doing fucking crunches and push-ups all day, all day long, push-ups and dips, then later at night the homeys would come and smoke weed at the garage of my building, and we'd do push-ups, push-ups, push-ups.

At that point I was going through issues with the mother of my older children. I had to leave culinary school to go work for my father. Misery can do one of two things for you—it can make you eat and be depressed, or it can make you be disciplined and work out. The good thing is, if you work out, once you break the misery, you're usually still working out.

So my man introduced me to the steroids, and I just went in. I fucking *went in*. I was on the juice, and I transformed my whole self, my whole life, my whole everything. I got happier, because I was fucking strong as fuck. Every day I wouldn't give a fuck, about her or my job or whatever, I'd just be in that gym every day and riding my bike every day by myself, just riding around, just in my own mind, you know?

I originally started going to the gym when I was thirteen or fourteen years old—and those were some hard-core New York gyms. I first worked out at this place called Mount Olympus on Northern Boulevard in Queens, I took the bus there. It was an underground gym; you know, a real strongman spot. It wasn't glamorous, it wasn't like the gyms people go to now, this was small-time shit. It was in the bottom half of a commercial building—you had to go through the parking lot entrance, walk down the slope for the cars, then come around to a room just a little bit bigger than an apartment, filled with a bunch of old equipment.

We started going there, me and my boys, because we all liked TV wrestling, and we wanted to get in shape like that. I'd loved watching wrestling since I was kid. I even used to rent a lot of the early UFC and WWF fights on VHS tapes from Blockbuster. I have a heritage of watching fights in my family, on both sides with both of my grandfathers—as an old-timer, you can bond with kids over that kind of thing. With my American grandfather, it was the old, bare-knuckle boxing era, and he had posters and even a statuette from some old fight. With my Albanian grandfather, it was modern-era fights, like Mike Tyson. And this wasn't WWF we watched but real wrestling, you know what I mean, you have to be in really good shape to real-wrestle, you have to make weight, do all kinds of crazy shit. Those who couldn't real-wrestle in school would makeshift wrestle, outside during football practice. But we were into the WWF stuff then, too—because this was the late 1990s, when everyone was into it.

At Mount Olympus it was me and my friend John Paul, and Rob Z. He was a fat fuck also, but he ended up losing mad weight and going into the marines,* and now

---

* 'Cause his father was a marine, but he was the type of kid who was always really good at war strategy games and stuff like that. And sometimes it's either that or you're in poverty. You want to just have a long-term thing that sets your family up—what else is going to do that? The military is what brought a lot of people out of impoverished situations.

he's an undercover cop. I think he's a narcotics officer, like a Donnie Brasco, which is kind of crazy, considering. I haven't seen him in a while, but the last time I saw him, he still looked good.

At Mount Olympus was our first sighting of a man taking steroids: there was this Chinese guy they called Bear, and he had pimples all over his back—which happens with steroids—but he was huge, so we thought he was ill. He was lifting weights, big ones, and he was a humongous guy. This was one of those gyms where monsters ago. There was this one Irish guy, so pale—you could see through this guy's skin, but he was the strongest guy. His legs were like fucking massive tree trunks. I'd never seen legs that big. He would always be in the front by the Myoplex, because when you lift you always have to have a shake. There was some hot women there, also, some babes, but there were mainly monsters.

We all loved going to the gym. It would really be like a hangout: People build relationships at the gym. You see people every day—you know, *Hey what's up, how you doin?* We would chill, do lots of people watching. You'd try to talk to women, you'd strike out . . . sometimes.

I know all the nuances of the gym. Mount Olympus was one of these gyms that a bodybuilder built. That's how a lot of these neighborhood gyms happen, some bodybuilder, they have their name and they take some of their winnings or whatever and they cop the fucking space. They put a gym there, and it becomes a space for people to go. Like, when I moved to the Bronx for a short period, me and Meyhem and his brother, Jay Steele, we would all go to this place called

Daro's Extreme Fitness. It was a crazy and legendary spot because it was where Victor Martinez went, the International Federation of Bodybuilding and Fitness pro. It was right off the Cross Bronx Expressway back then, just take a left on White Plains Road. It was just a storefront at that point, and it was sick, like full of old-ass men in there, sweaty, but it was a dope place to work out.

I also went for a bit to this place called Lost Battalion Hall, a city recreation center in Rego Park right next to Goldfingers, the famous strip club on Queens Boulevard that got closed by the cops and became a Burger King. I was actually scouted to lift as a kid, by my old baseball coach Lenny Waxman. His son Sean was a powerlifter for Team USA—he was either in the Olympics or an alternate, something like that. They always thought I'd be good at lifting, too, and they went to Lost Battalion Hall. Every neighborhood should have a Lost Battalion Hall. It's like a YMCA run by the city, with a pool and basketball and everything, but they also had powerlifting and they had a boxing gym with a Russian powerlifting coach, like a sick dude. There were really serious powerlifters who went there, and they would train the more advanced boxers at that gym—some champion Golden Gloves boxers came out of that place. I went there for a little bit, and learned how to squat, but I didn't want to go into some gym with my old baseball coach—that just felt weird, so I had to raise up out of that.

That neighborhood was Russian, and still is. Over there on Northern Boulevard near Mount Olympus, it was all Greek and Italian dudes at the gym, and then as you go north and get closer to Bayside and Rego Park and then hit Forest Hills, you're going to find the Bukharan Russians at the gym.

I also had a membership at the Platinum Health Club in Forest Hills. It was right on Queens Boulevard, and it was open twenty-four hours a day, and the Bukharan Russians used to work out there heavy. This dude Gino, who just passed away, owned it, and he was also a pro bodybuilder. Now it's closed—it became a Russian supermarket. There, the Russians would all be wearing all-white Diesel, with crazy cologne on, in sunglasses doing lat rows; you know, doing crazy movements in full club regalia. They were dressed like they were ready to go to the fucking club at any second. Most of the time they weren't even working out, they'd just be out in front of the place smoking cigarettes, or just fucking around like it was a social club. They'd chill, they'd talk to one dude, do one pull-up, then leave and go about their day.

Bukharans, every two seconds, they're saying *suka blyat*, which in Bukharian means something like "fucking bitch," or "piece of shit," or "fuck your mother." If you're a Bukharan tough guy, that's at the end of every sentence. I mean, if you grew up in Queens and you knew somebody Bukharan, you would know what *suka blyat* meant without even knowing *what* it meant, because that's the one thing they're saying that you can pick up on. That's the type of shit you always understand.*

---

* I feel like I can understand situations in any language—because I can read people, unless they are really fucking good at disguising what they're saying. Sometimes I can even talk back. I can speak Spanish pretty well, thanks to my days in the restaurant kitchen, and Spanish accents are much easier for me to understand. French is harder, because I don't know it yet, and it is extremely fancy, like just for a little pencil, it's like *blah blah blah blah blah*—so many words.

I was also obsessed with the way this one Bukharan dude who worked the counter said *vanilla*. I was like, *Yo, let me get a Myoplex shake.* He'd go, *Do you want WANEELA?*

It sounded like he was gargling, like he was strangling. It was ridiculous, and I was obsessed with ordering a *WANEELA* shake with a banana in it and some extra protein, just to hear him say it. You drink it and it leaves your mouth feeling like you just ate chalk—because you did, pretty much.

The Platinum gym was the heart of the Steroid Years for me. And I liked those years. It was a masculine time: I felt like a man; you know, shooting all kinds of steroids, just being a beast in the gym. We would be squatting without shoes on and getting powder everywhere. Screaming at each other, hitting the machines. We used to go nuts, throwing weights around like fucking animals. They'd ask us to stop and we'd say, *Get the fuck outta here.*

But mainly I was there to focus on my bod. I would put my headphones on and hit the crunches every single day. Every time I walked in the gym, I would go right to the sit-up thing and do as many sit-ups as I could, then go hit the leg press thing just as hard. I did stupid leg presses: I would find every single weight in the fucking house and load it on the leg press machine—one-hundred-pound plates on each side, as many as will fit, all the forty-five-pound plates. And then the motherfucker would sit on top of the machine . . . and I'd be, *Ahhhhh, ughhh.* I could leg press well over 1,500 pounds then. It wasn't like I was doing biceps, or triceps, or, like, butterfly curls on the machine. I'm not that type of lifter. We're talking lifting iron, moving some serious iron: bench press, squat, dead lift, shoulder press, heavy-duty movements with the long bars and the big weights, just up and down. I used to do a lot of fucking weight, man. I'm short and compact, you know, but I'm strong.

During the Steroid Years there would be times where we'd go into the gym every morning at around ten o'clock. I would ride my bike to work at a restaurant in Forest Hills, and after work I'd ride my bike to the gym, go late night, and then ride home, too. I wasn't even thin then, I was just strong as fuck. Damn, was I strong. And I was determined. I've always had a certain amount of ability for a husk, a husky boy. And of course I was also on some shit, as in steroids. We would usually shoot up in the alley behind the gym.

During those years, I became obsessed with this vision of what I should look like, what I wanted to look like. Growing up, looking at all types of people that are in shape, or fucking bodybuilders, and just wondering, like, *Why the hell aren't we the same?* You just become obsessed with looking the same way, at trying all the ways to get there. That's why cosmetic surgery and makeup and all those things are such a fucking big business. People want to look good. And steroids are still a huge business, a big underground business.

I got onto it from a friend who has been doing it since he was in high school, who knew a dude we called Muscle Head Ed, and this fuck introduced a lot of people to steroids. My friend was in mad good shape—he was strong and huge, with a fucking little-ass waist. You know, just, it's all about genetics. I wasn't born with the little-waist genetics, and he was. So steroids just kind of helps you: it helps you when you have really good genetics, it helps you when you have shitty genetics, but it doesn't get you to where someone who has the better genetics would be.

I shot the juice because I always wanted to be fucking six feet tall and fucking huge. I'm five-seven if I'm lucky, and I'm just wide the other way. I wanted to be like Arnold. I wanted to be like Ronnie Coleman. I wanted to be a massive fucking musclehead, for some reason . . . I don't know why. No, I do know why: I wanted to intimidate. I never wanted to be looked at as a punk, so I thought muscles, and me being strong, would make it work. I got strong, but I never really got the muscles.

All I wanted to do then was lift heavy-ass weights and look at myself in the mirror. When you're on steroids, you become obsessed with the mirror. It's not like I had mad cuts, but you just see things—it's like a mirage. You know when you start getting muscles because the muscle pushes the vein out of the skin, that's the telltale sign you're getting buff. I would do mad fucking workouts, then go look in the mirror: *Yo, see the vein, bro?* You do half your set, look in the mirror to see your pump. Go get a drink from the water fountain, look at your pump again. You always got to look at your pump. What's the point of going to the gym if you can't look at your pump?

Lifting weights is a big booster, no matter your shape. You know, you look at yourself doing it and monitor yourself making strides. When you start building a little chest, then you start poking it out a little bit and feeling better about yourself. You're stronger, you can fucking lift heavy-ass shit.

I would suggest powerlifting for anybody who wants to feel better about themselves. Having the power to lift something is sexy, that's what I'm saying.

At one point I was really in on it: all I wanted to do was lift, lift heavy-ass weights and look at myself in the mirror. Not like I was really adding mad cuts, like I told you, but I could feel the changes, I could tell it was coming. You start seeing certain things form—it's like, *Oh, okay, let's go.*

It takes a week or so after you do steroids the first time, and then you start feeling it in your workouts. Maybe you feel a little sharper, too—maybe it's all mental. You can take an Advil and stop feeling pain, but does that mean it is really working? Or are you just telling yourself that? We don't really know.

At that point I was taking all kinds of things. I took the Ephedra, which is now illegal. It cooks your intestines and your internal organs, but you lose mad weight, it makes you burn mad fat. You sweat a lot. I used to get it at GNC before it was illegal. I also took this thing called Xenedrine that was sold on TV—the "hydroxy cut," a multivitamin slash fat burner. Hell yeah, I took that shit, I took that shit for thirty days and I drank mad water. In addition, I was taking the steroids: I was taking Decdan, testo, trenbolone acetate, and Sustanon. Oh my god, and Winstrol and D-Bal, for fuck's sake. All the things that end in *L*.

There was an asthma one that would open your lungs, it made you mad vascular. A lot of juice was shot in that bathroom of the Platinum gym, and in the alley just behind it. There was no need to do it in the alley: we just liked to do it in the outside air. I once shot steroids in front of my mother.

She found the needles, and she was so confused, she didn't know what was happening.

You want me to tell you the truth? Everything I learned about steroids was from Mark McGwire doing steroids. When they found out androstenedione was in his locker room, I went to GNC and I bought some. I was taking it every day, every other day, maybe. There's a regimen for steroids, a schedule. It's probably different for everybody, but there's definitely a specific technique. I was definitely abusing steroids, and I was doing it wrong. I don't think I did it right, for sure.

But I did it because you want to fucking go maximum, right? You've made a decision. You're going to shoot yourself with a needle, you're going to go gung ho, you're going to go in. It's like a whole program. In fact it's *The Program*. It's a movie about college football—one of my first mixed tapes is named after it. There's one character called Lattimer, who fucking gets his piss exchanged in his bladder with a catheter. The NCAA must have been wild back then. There are some sketchy parts to his character. He's roided out, and he breaks car windows with his head and throws a woman halfway across the room, a college girl, and he gets accused of rape. They have to take him off the roids, he gets run over at the goal line, he goes back on the roids, the coach finds out. Later on Lattimer sits on the bench crying, his face paint running down—he knows he can't make the NFL without the roids.

When you're doing steroids, you definitely feel like you're bigger than you are. You feel mad swollen: you walk with your arms out a little bit, even when they're not that big.

Then when you stop, you deflate. Your brain deflates also: you're like a crybaby, crying in the car in the rain. During the Steroid Years, I was an emotional wreck.

That wasn't why I stopped, to be honest. I had to stop lifting weights after I had my first hernia surgery: I did it deadlifting. I popped it deadlifting, and that shit is fucking painful, the worst.

After the surgery, that's when I just started doing dips and going crazy with a workout routine right in front of my house.

There were two pillars that protected a pay phone right on the street in front of where I lived; it was the perfect height for me to do dips on. You raise your legs and you just go down, down and up, down and up, working your arms like crazy. I would have my little flip phone—I would play my little music on YouTube—and place it right on top of the pay phone. I had my lineman gloves; you know, offensive linemen have those gloves, they're all padded on the hands. People would walk back and forth around me.

That thing in front of my building was a thing for years. I used to do dips like you couldn't believe, two hundred, two hundred and fifty dips every day. Push-ups nonstop, but no pull-ups, I'm not good at that, I did more dips instead. I'd go downstairs to go to the little store across the street, I'd do dips. Crossed the street on the way back, did 'em again. Left the house, walked to the park, I did 'em. Left the park, did 'em. Sometimes I would just chill there all day at the fucking pay phone with my flip phone playing music. I'd go down late at night and do it again in the morning. Whenever I was outside, I did it. It was a ritual.

Then I saw other motherfuckers doing it, too. I was at 229 pounds and shredded. Well, not really shredded, but for me, it was shredded.

Then they just took the whole pay phone away. There's no replacement: it was the perfect height for me, the perfect arm placement. There's other things that are protecting phones elsewhere, but I've never found one the same size. It was a major blow.

But that's not a great reason for why I stopped working out: really, I just stopped doing it; you just stop doing things. I had quit smoking weed after my hernia surgery for a minute, but then I started working out and smoking, and then the smoking kind of took over the working out, just a little bit more. I like working out, I like doing activities that are physical, I do enjoy it—but, man, I like smoking a lot. I like to get high, I will never apologize for that. You can do both. People get lazy in life; you know, you don't always follow through with every single thing. And there's so many things to do in life, you have to make choices.

And I don't want to ever, ever, ever catch another hernia, I've gotten one twice, and last time it put me out of work for weeks. The hernia really fucked me up.

The last time I got one, as I have told the story before, I was in Alaska just a few years ago—I was in Alaska for a total of eight days, when I was supposed to be there for four. I had to immediately cancel whatever else I had left for the year, and I couldn't do anything strenuous for six weeks. I worked out then, but my performances at that point were even more physical. I couldn't jump in the crowd, or have anybody hit me in the stomach, or anything like that.

Hernias are actually one of the most common sports injuries there are, period. It's easily fixable, but I don't know if you've seen on TV, you know the lawyer helpline, they had something literally about hernia mesh malfunctioning, and what do you think happened to me? My hernia mesh malfunctioned, and it was put in between the dates on the commercial. I'm not going to be part of the suit, but my mesh broke within two months of getting it the first time, and I finally got it fixed for good when I was doing that show in Alaska. The surgeon there* told me that the hole was that big and the original doctor only used the piece that was this big. So the Alaskan doctor put a piece that big, and I've been fine ever since, at least three years now. It's made out of surgical stainless steel, which is probably the fucking reason they have to put their hands along my penis every time I go through security.

But I don't really miss the gym. Gyms ain't the same as they used to be—it's all like mad fitness gear and Pelotons and Pilates and shit like that. All of the little old-school gyms, they're mostly not there anymore, you know.† But mainly

---

* I went to the emergency room at Providence Medical Center, which is an incredible hospital. As soon as I walked in, I saw some lady—shirtless, titties flapping—with a needle in her arm, screaming, *I need my drugs. I just need a little bit, why are you doing this to me?* She tried to bite the security guard. This is the first thing I saw. I was like, *Aight.* Then I see some people drunk out of their minds on the floor. And then I'm like, *Yeah, this is going to be a trip.* The doctor came in. She was trying to calm me down, but she couldn't get my hernia back in, either. They did a CAT scan on the lower half of my body, and it was apparently entangled in my valve and intestine, so they needed to do an emergency procedure right away. The doctor was one of the best, in fact—I got lucky.

† I did recently pump a small amount of iron at this old-school gym called Frenchie's on Broadway in Brooklyn with a bodybuilder named John Baseman. Frenchie, a former bodybuilder and wrestling ref, died not too long after that, may he rest in peace.

I'm just not in that life anymore. I already know how much weight I can lift, I don't need to find that out. I'm not trying to fucking be the strongest man in the world and lift heavy weights anymore, and end up with a little waist. I'll never have a little waist. I don't look in the mirror and hope to see somebody else.

Explosion Movements

So look, obviously I've been up and down in weight my entire life. Up and down, up and down. But I've always been a husk, I've always had this shape. Back in 2000, I was 230 pounds—I was in shape. I was strong, but I still had this body. To be honest, I don't even look at a scale anymore.

We're all built in certain ways, and that's why we look like certain shapes. Body structure, man, everyone has that different shit. Really, all of us are shaped weird, when you think about it. Some people might have very thin legs and an ass that's a fatty, or a rounder. There are people with huge stomachs, like I know people who just can't see anything when they look down. There are some people who only have huge asses, like weirdly huge asses, and then a little waist and legs. They look thin when they're sitting down, and when they get up, it's like a fucking huge spare tire on there. We once knew a girl in junior high school who had that body, and we heard she became a hooker, a woman of the night, and then later, she became a person of the church.

My form is pretty strong up top, then I get more thick by the thigh. I have thick, big legs and I have a flat ass. I have a little stomach hangage, but it's a normal level of hangage. My stomach isn't as protruding as another fat man's, but I'm wide. I just somehow collected all this fat on my love handles, like a muffin ass, a muffin top. I have one big love handle, and you know, I'm a box, a square. But I'm a fucking strong square.

I love my shape, also. I want you to know that. I think I have a great shape. I mean, obviously I am three hundred fucking pounds and I'm a square. But I think I look gorgeous, like the shining light in this fucking bitter world.

I honestly didn't even know I was fat, when I was younger. I thought I was just husky. The part of the store where I bought my shirts was called Husky, and that's what my mom would always call me, that or hefty: *You're a hefty boy.*

And I was. My thighs used to get so violently rashed in my youth that I had a special pair of biker shorts that I had to wear just to separate them. My legs were creamed and powdered under the biker shorts, like I was a piece of chicken. My mom actually pulled out a measuring tape from her purse the other day—she said she had been carrying it around since I was a little kid so she could measure my thighs when she was buying me pants. But I wasn't ever embarrassed: I just decided to not care what people thought; to see how it was funny. That's the art of it—when my mom had to do that, I just thought it was funny. Like I said, I had a sick confidence.

I wasn't embarrassed then and I'm not embarrassed now because that's growing pains. Maybe most people would be mortified. It's a mortifying thing. But I'm built different. They don't build 'em like me. I say, don't give a shit if you're embarrassed about certain things. Make yourself laugh. Who's making fun of me? I don't care, go fuck yourself.

That's also what makes your skin thick—when you're not what the world thinks you should be, when you grow up a chunky, husky boy. That's also how you become a fucking better human being. I knew early on that maybe you think you look funny; you just have to love yourself extra hard. Like I said before, my mom taught me that.

So I wasn't one of those guys that wore their fucking T-shirt all the time at the beach—it gets so fucking long, you're nearly drowning in it. You're a little overweight. So?

You got to just always remember, they'll laugh, but it'll be okay. Sometimes shit's just funny. You got to think about yourself like, *Damn, I'm at the beach. It's ninety degrees and I'm wearing a fucking black T-shirt down to my knees in the water. What am I really doing? Take the fucking shirt off, kid.* I mean, you were there while you ate all the hamburgers and french fries. You knew you were going to go to the beach. You knew you didn't have to do that. You could have fucking got on the bike. You could have played a little bit more ball. You didn't need to eat pizza three times that day. Which I did. Of course: I lived across the street from the pizzeria. What do you think I ate every day?*

I like to think I have the body of a bovine, an oxen. I don't have a long torso and I have a shorter limb, but my center of gravity is good, and my ass and thighs are all muscle. My legs and my hamstrings and my quads have this balance and strength and the ability to provide a strong push. And I'm built fucking tight—I'm a tight package, proportioned in the middle, that square, I have the power of the short and stout.

So I'm good at squats. I'm good at benching. I'm good at shoulder pressing. Back when I did leg presses, I leg pressed the entire rack, as many weights as you can put on, like twelve hundred, fifteen hundred pounds. And that was

---

* I also lived across the street from the Chinese food restaurant. I grew up on Chinese food. Wonton soup was my favorite thing in the world. Sometimes, I would go and get it without the soup, just the wontons. And you want to know what's even sicker? Sometimes I would just eat the noodle from around the meat. One of the reasons I know a good wonton now is because they made a good one. Of course, I also grew up on fucking kung pao chicken, sesame chicken, General Tso's chicken, chicken and broccoli. We're talking about the young days, when my mother would order food for me.

even without steroids. I'm not great at stuff that has to do with having long arms or an incredible grip, because I have smaller hands. I have an artistic hand, though, I can hold the fuck out of some shit. I was born not just with a short center of gravity, but also with a superior fucking knack to draw guys with guns and with fucking army outfits on.*

They say that when you're a football scout, you're often looking at the guys that have the more muscular ass, dudes that have the lower body like me. You just have the fucking ass going into the hamstring where the gluteus muscles are really strong, and then the hamstring muscles, that's like ... power. Not for all positions, but athletically, that's where defensive players and, like, skill players often generate their power. These are the people that run and jump and do fast, explosive movements.

Even as I write this, as I take a quick break to roll to the trash can in my office chair, I am not being lazy—I had to push off with my leg. Remember that: I still had to do an athletic move. I did a fast-twitch muscle movement, an explosion movement. I did. That's what I've been working on, I've been working on my explosion movements.

You just have to find your own movements for your own shape: whatever movement you enjoy doing the most. Everyone is good at at least one movement. Maybe you like squatting a lot, or chair dancing. You may not think you are good at any movement. Remember how I told you before: you have to believe that you can do anything, then you just go for it.

* My aunt once said she was surprised I became a rapper because she thought I would be an artist, not a singer, since I could draw so well when I was growing up.

And you could even be fucking Vinny Testaverde, who's almost like an out-of-shape, rounded guy, but still be a good quarterback. As long as you have that arm, you know? Even Tom Brady isn't shredded and thin—he's still kind of rounded—and he's the best ever. And if we're talking about overcoming physical obstacles: Jim Abbott was born with one hand, and he throws pitches in the Major League.

Maybe I'm not meant to be thin, or to be the world's strongest man. Maybe I was meant to be an artist, to draw. I was meant to perform, to sing and dance. I can honestly say I dance for a living: I have danced in front of 55,000 people in the rugby stadium in Johannesburg, on Eminem's Marshall Mathers tour. I was literally dancing in the light South African rain, singing and dancing.

You know, they did a survey and they said that dad bods are more attractive to women than six-pack abs, anyway. This is another point: How could anyone be so dedicated to their abs? If abs are the whole basis of everything in your life, you're fucked up in the head. You're not a normal person and you're not a fun person if all you care about is how many reps you've done in your abs; you're a fuck boy or girl. Then you're constantly telling everyone about your crunches.

I just did a thousand crunches. Yeah, I gotta do ten thousand more crunches today. Somebody calls. What are you doing? *Yeah, I was just doing some crunches. It's three o'clock, gotta do some more leg raises.*

The world forces us to believe that we are always supposed to look a certain way. Even doctors and science tell you that, that you'll live longer, if you do this or look like that. But all these people who do it, they fucking do all these things to look that certain way, and they're not even all that happy.

And nobody totally loves their shape. I remember back in the day I went to a taping of *The Maury Povich Show* over on Thirty-Fourth Street. The first episode was Jack Hanna with the animals, and the second was "I Hate Myself, I Am So Ugly." And then it was all these fit women wearing little miniskirts. It was ridiculous, it was total garbage, but it just goes to show you everybody has an issue with their shape. Nobody likes the way they look. Everybody has the good mirror and the bad mirror, the one that makes you look like a can of tuna fish.

Still, I don't know why some fat guys with the stomach wear their stomach tucked into their pants. I don't know where their waist is supposed to be, but it ain't there. On the thin man, yes, the waist is around the belly button, usually. But no one thin wears their pants there, either. You wear the pants down around toward your hips; you know, just so it's covering your ass crack. I just think it's bizarre when you try to stuff your stomach into pants. What's that about? I don't know. And then you have this fucking FUPA area underneath the waistline where it's just like a little punching bag in the pubic area. You just want to punch it.

I mean, some dudes, they have that really overhanging thing, an actual flap. It is a tough choice to tuck or not to tuck that, because that is going to look weird no matter what. Let it hang, then you have a long shirt to cover it. But no matter what, with a stomach you have to make choices. Are you going to be the guy that tucks his stomach into the pants and then also tucks the shirt into the pants over the stomach? That's fucking crazy.

A little gentle compression might be okay. Spandex must feel amazing to wear, but for many men it's just not an option.

You could choose to Lululemon your stomach. The Lululemons are the leggings that fake everybody out. Some people tie corsets so that their waists are as small as possible. And then when they're home they let go: it's like, poof! Everything falls out. Spanish women have been wearing something like that for years, it's called a *faja*, a full body girdle, almost like compression socks. They are tighter on your thighs, to make your ass fat in a certain way. It probably takes hours to get tucked into the fucking thing. Like, 100 percent, if they put me in the faja, I would look like a totally different person. But hell no would I do that, though, because stuffing shit in a faja don't work. It's still there, it's just stuffed somewhere.

I prefer a good pair of long ball shorts; you know, basketball shorts. Straight up, the boxers underneath, because it's comfortable. In fact, I wear similarly shaped modified swimming trunks every single day.

When you're purposely overly thin, it's ridiculous. Like models, you fucking let people take pictures of you while you wear clothes, and you despise food. Like that's your fucking life. What the hell is that? It's very weird to me. My first fashion show, I went with a bandage on my head, and I sat next to a supermodel who was born in 1995, when I was already carrying a knife and wearing Timberlands. Fashion shows are *Zoolander* shit, I'm telling you.

I think that's all much weirder than having love handles or a big stomach flap.

And all those salad bowl places the thin people eat at? Personalizing your salad is such an asshole, pompous thing to do. I can only imagine that people who go in there, they don't like food. It's like a rabbit dispensary of little fucking food pellets to a little hamster in the fucking glass box. Come into the glass box and get your little pellets. And there's always, like, steps: Step one, pick your bowl, step two, would you like mesclun or mixed greens? Step three, go fuck yourself.

I mean, I'm not saying to fucking stuff yourself till you can't walk out of the room, Walter Hudson–style shit. You remember that back in the day? He was one of the first people we ever heard about having to be airlifted out of the fucking room. They had to cut a hole—use the jaws of life. Oh my god, that shit makes you sad. That's not a life, that's a science experiment, to see how far you can go before you hurt yourself.

Fuck It, I'll Start Tomorrow

So, I do want to weigh less. What, are you serious? I fucking want to lose mad weight. I might not be doing anything right this exact second, but, you know, you try, and you have it in your mind. If you're husky, you're always dieting in your mind. I always think about not drinking soda and not eating dessert or bad shit. Every day, I think about it, and I often do it. I drink water and I *monitor*. I fucking pour the soda that I got because somebody brought it over into the sink, 'cause that's what I gotta do. I won't say I didn't taste it, though.

Most of my life, I don't know if it's so much of a diet I've been doing, you know what I'm saying? When I was a really little kid I wasn't thinking about what I was eating too much of. I was thinking about Matchbox cars and G.I. Joes and eating whatever was around, whatever I actually liked the taste of. When I was a little older, still a growing boy, it was just, you try not to eat hamburgers every day. You try not to eat bagels every day. That's a start. I would think to myself, like, *Maybe don't have a bagel today. Don't eat a bagel.* Or maybe, have a bagel today, but then, *Why are you having another piece of bread with cheese? Why are you eating the entire bread now?* Now the salami is gone.

Now you're asking your grandmother for something. She would be like, *Eh, you just ate, c'mon.* But then she would give it to me because I'd act like a little fucking biatch. That's why. Another reason why she would always make me food is because she wanted me to eat the good Albanian stuff: the peppers and tomatoes. The good *pite*, and her chicken and rice. She didn't want me to eat hamburger, hamburger, hamburger, bagel, bagel, bagel. That's what my grandmother would always say to me, with her Albanian accent. And *bagel with the cheese. Bagel with the cheese.*

You know, my Albanian side of the family, there's no issue with food like this, because they come from famine. No one was worried or thinking about overeating or dieting because before, there was no fucking food to overeat. Their cuisine was peasant food; you know, creating things from what you have—flour into all kinds of doughy shit, beans, the bones from lamb meat. Tomatoes and shit, and spinach and, like, wild dandelion greens in the backyard. When I visited my grandmother in Skopje, she just picked a bunch of shit from back there, and baked it in the *pite*. You're poor, you eat fucking beans and bread and broth and wild greens, and that's it.

After my grandparents moved out of our apartment when I was around twelve—that's when my mom started in with the hide-and-seek games with food.

In my teenage years, many things needed to be hidden in my house. You know what I mean—if you have a hefty boy, you got to hide the cookies and the peanut butter and the chocolate chips, especially if you need it to make a cheesecake. My mom was a baker, so she had to fucking put stuff underneath other stuff so I wouldn't find it.* My mom

---

* I could really write a whole book on ingenuity-type things, tactics, a survival guide for snacking in houses without snacks. In a time of need, let me tell you what else I've gone to: opening up the Swiss Miss hot chocolate packages and eating the marshmallows out of them. That's what you stoop to. Then you dip a finger into the chocolate. These are desperation moves—disgusting desperation moves. I'm just talking about the times where you're having a sugar breakdown and you just fucking flip out. You need something; you know, like even an apple and peanut butter. Listen, if there's an apple, peanut butter, and hot sauce in my house, I'm lit—all those three things together. I mean, that's actually a healthy sweet snack. Plus, I usually go to Whole Foods and get that ground-up peanut butter, when they grind it up to order: I get honey-roasted, or almond butter. The hot sauce is optional, I just like to put that twist on it, it just freaks me out a little bit, it counterbalances things.

would put them in the microwave. That was a useful one for a little bit, but then I'd get hip to that. So it would go in the oven, underneath the pans that are always stored in there in New York City. My mother's gone so far as to hide them in her room, in closets, in coats, in the arm of a jacket, a panel in the flooring.

And of course, my mother tried to hide things from me in the fridge. You can't hide it in the fridge—nothing can be hidden from me in the fridge. I'm taking everything out, and then I'm putting everything back in. The rustling sounds of opening bags, the nonstop opening of the fridge? That was me. Most of the time if you need me, I'm in the fridge area.

Even today I'm actually guarding the fridge most of the time, I set up my workspace right in front of the fridge, at both my home and my studio, so that if anyone needs to fucking get to it, that person needs to see me first.

Back then, my mom was always paying attention to what she ate. I think she was gorgeous. She was a catch—she was on some Cher shit back then, with long black curls. She thought she was chubby when she was growing up, and it stuck with her. And definitely being an American woman, and growing up in the society that made women very conscious about what they look like and having to be a certain size to be accepted in the society at that time. Who knows what the fuck was instilled in them at that point in time?

My mom is cool enough not to buy into all that society shit, and as I've talked about many times before, she loved to eat new things and explore and cook, and we did all of that together. She is amazing. But there was always some sort of situation going on with her, she was always, you know, "watching herself."

We'd make broiled burgers on whole wheat and these baked sweet potato fries with crushed red pepper and garlic I still love; a pasta salad with grilled chicken and broccoli and vinaigrette I still love.* We'd blot the pizza, remove the cheese, we'd blot all the fat from the burger as it cooked, blot, blot, blot. I use that trick with a lot of things, like if something has too much oil you just take it out with a piece of Bounty, right from the pan. I always use Bounty—it's the quicker picker upper.

My mother also taught me the art of throwing food away so you can't eat anymore. Throw the kung pao chicken in the trash, put water on top of it. I took it further: spit in the lo mein, the General Tso's. It's sick. And sometimes it doesn't even work. If the food is just thrown away and is right on top of the trash can? That's an easy pick.

I think one of the only real diets I ever did in my life was Atkins, a long time back. You were straight-up allowed to eat sausage and bacon, cheese and eggs—mostly protein. I did it for three weeks, and I lost forty pounds in those three weeks.

I kept it off for a week. It comes right back because it's fake weight loss. You eat one piece of bread and it's over, it's a wrap. Plus, when you're on it, you shit like a fucking pig, like a fucking animal. It's despicable. Everything comes out

---

* I call it the Old World pasta salad. It's old news, but I still do it all the time. We used to take it to Jones Beach when I was growing up. My mother had everything in a big-ass bag—she had cutlery, paper plates, sauce, seasoning, everything in that big-ass bag. My mother's known for bags. I think there was one that was a floral bag, and then there was one that was slightly denim-looking. It was huge, you know, you slung it over the shoulder. You could carry a full-sized dog in it. Hundred percent you could put my bigger dog Gigi in there, plus an umbrella.

of you at once. You can't even go anywhere like that, you can't work out like that. I am glad Dr. Atkins died a horrible death, because he fucking made people sick. He died from being on Atkins. You're in something called ketosis: your fucking body is eating the fat away, but it is also eating muscle, so it makes you a frumpy fuck, and then you try to work out and you shit yourself and you have no energy. I was just like, *Damn, I might as well just eat some bread.*

The hottest new thing in dieting now is the fasting where you're not technically fasting, you just don't eat for most of a whole day. I just don't feel you get optimum performance out of your body when you fast, if you're doing any kind of physical activity or thinking. You get light-headed and fucking loopy and weird. Maybe sometimes good art comes from that feeling. But not everyone's an artist. Sometimes you need to go do a fucking one-hundred-page architectural report on a Japanese building, you know?

It's been a long time since I was on an actual diet, but as I said, you're still always dieting in your mind, if you're like me. I'm like, *Damn, you know, I need to be healthy.* Your mind is like, *Nah, don't do it. Don't eat the bagel.* But then your body is yearning for it, so you give in to the carnal lust of the food.

And think about how hard that is for me. Food is what I do.

So for me it's always *Fuck it, I'll start tomorrow.* But, you know, tomorrow never comes. I was talking to my friend about how you always have to start your diet "tomorrow." But tomorrow always has to be on Monday—you have to start fresh in the week. You can't start a diet on a Tuesday or on Wednesday, that can't be tomorrow. Tomorrow can't be on a

Friday, because you want the weekend. You want the weekend for your last hurrah.

I have had a lot of last hurrahs with ice cream and sodas, and like a drunk or a drug addict, I go out with a bang . . . I mean, I have a last hurrah every day in my mind. I'm always like, *Ah, this is the last fucking ice cream.* In my mind, I'm like, *Yo, I've got to really do this, you know?* And then I end up waking up in the middle of the night and having ice cream, or in the morning I'll think, *I'll just have a taste.* We're the type of people that have to, you know, get the ice cream, take a couple scrapes, or whatever it is you do with an ice cream.

And it's not like I am even looking for the newest diet to do. I know what to eat every day. I went to culinary school; I made a 100 in nutrition. My body maybe doesn't show it, but I know what the fuck nutrition is about. I know what you need to have. I know what's really good, what's wholesome.

I love to roast carrots, cauliflower, potatoes, garlic whole, altogether on a little tray. That's banging, fucking thirty minutes in the toaster oven, everything's crunchy and gorgeous. A little olive oil, salt, lemon. You can lose weight if you cook like that, clean as fuck. Olive oil, lemons, avocados, and shit like that.

Balkan delights like I grew up with are usually healthy, too, except when it's a baked-dough kind of good. Other than the most famous of dishes, the *pite*, the *burek*, everything else is pretty healthy. All the side dishes, the beans and cucumbers and tomatoes, the wild greens and peppers and tomatoes. Those are my go-tos. Most of what I eat at home is wholesome. It's healthy-ish. I pound out a chicken breast, thin. Fry it in olive oil, a shallow fry with a shitload of onion, and yellow and red pepper. Then I put cilantro in there, garlic, a ton of cherry tomatoes, and these marinated olives that I found that are a mixture of red and black olives. A squeeze of lemon and more fresh cilantro at the end to reinforce that flavor. That's a mean-ass dish, I'll tell you that.

I also put mad homemade chicken cutlets in a cold pasta dish, with balsamic, a lot of garlic, roasted red peppers, cherry tomatoes, basil, fresh muzzarelle, black pepper, and good olive oil. Then toss it with pasta—I prefer the tennis racket shape, the racchette. How many chicken cutlets is mad chicken cutlets? I like to have an abundant amount of chicken cutlets in there, like four, and I pound them thin, so it's a lot of chicken cutlet. But I like to make a lot of salad, because it's fucking really good cold or room temperature, and it lasts forever, for days. It gets better as it sits.

It's not low calorie, it's not even low fat. But it's healthy. Yes, it is fried chicken, but it's better than if I ordered a fried chicken sandwich somewhere, and that's how we should compare it—against the worst of the worst bad food you would have eaten otherwise. If you're going to fucking decide to have this or to have that, then this is still healthy. It's a wholesome snack. We're using a good animal. We're using good products. When you use the best products that other people take care to raise and put passion and love into, it's different from putting something into your body that is machine made or was processed.

I just had occasion to try an Impossible Whopper, and it was quite delicious. It hit the spot—I felt like I was eating something really bad for me, that tasted so good. But was it in all actuality good for me? We don't know. We have no idea what this stuff is, what it is made out of. It just burst into the scene, you know? That's why I'd rather just eat good vegetables, made really well. I don't need to be tricked into eating chicken nuggets that are made out of some bullshit. I know this is kind of cheesy, but we need to discuss the importance of a plant-based diet. Give me a nice piece of broccoli, a piece of cauliflower. Eat all the vegetables, every single one of them, try them, cook them in different ways. My motto is just drown them in olive oil.

I try to not eat processed shit now, but you know, being on the road as a musician or working on a TV show, the road life, that's not an easy life, especially a middle-of-America road life.

When you're on tour for days with nothing around but truck stops and miles and miles of nothing, you don't have a lot of options when you're starving. You're eating all kinds of fucking bullshit at all times, at different times of night. It's so fucking hard to stay on any type of regimen whatsoever. You're just scavenging, eating whatever the hell is there.

It's nasty shit, though. You see those rotating hot dogs. For some reason that hot dog and the thing that's coated in breading, and the taquitos and the egg rolls are all rotating on the same heating apparatus, but that's not the right way to heat these things. They're not crisping, and they'll just be there all day.

Most of the time when you go into the rest stop store, even if you have no intention of having anything, you cruise, peruse, you always have to try a snack. Try every flavor chip that you've never had before. All the different Sour Patch

Kids around, and all kinds of shit. You'll just see these fucking truckers just filling up on sixty-four-ounce jugs of soda.

I remember I was knocked out on a recent trip, and when I woke up we were at a little-ass gas station in the middle of who the fuck knows, I don't even remember where it was. I don't even know where we were, all I know is that the lady serving us had a *Fargo*-style voice, and she told me that she was going to gamble in St. Louis or some shit, like an hour away from where she was right at that gas station, and that was a big trip for her.

The only thing they had available from the menu was tater tots. Then the lady, she was like, *Ohooo, hold on one second, we'll check*, and she went to the back. *Oh,* she said after she came back, *we have one package of chicken fingers left!* So that was our options, tater tots and one package of chicken fingers.

So on tour, you know, like almost every other day there was an item from a fast-food place—an apple pie, a nugget. I only like single burgers from McDonald's,* without cheese, and two is my limit. Some McDonald's are better than others. Bad McDonald's is standard when in Europe. When you're on tour, McDonald's is always open, anywhere you are. I recently had late-night bad McDonald's in Valencia,

---

* And, I'll admit, it's not just on tour when I ate fast food. One day when I left my studio to go home, my girlfriend, Val, asked me to bring two slices of pizza home on the way, but instead I just ordered a pie to the house. But before I got the pie for her, I also went to McDonald's. I got one hamburger, one small fry, and a six-piece nugget that I later threw out. I'm lying, I ate one. I had the burger, and I ate the fries like an animal, but it was a small fries, it was like ten fries. And then I went home and I had one slice of pizza.

Spain. There was a crack whore there, cursing us out 'cause we didn't want any of her crack mouth. Then she found the guy who did as we were driving away. We turned to look, and there she was blowing him in the alley, just as I was eating a cheeseburger, a bad one.

But on one of my early tours, we were all like, *We're not eating anything bad this time. We're not doing nothing fucking bad.*

This was the European tour, and we had a bus, and I made Vice buy me a blender. I'd bought a food processor. We went to the fucking store in the UK, a big, humongous Target-like type of place, with food and shit. This was on the Mr. Wonderful tour in 2015, when I had just signed to Vice. Vice paid for the bus, too. This was the early days, and I was the man there. They loved me. The homey Eddy Moretti, he was still the president of content, and he was the guy. He okayed all the checks, and they were bountiful.

I was also in really good shape at that point. I was looking real good. I was still 275 to 280 pounds, but in fighting shape. At that point I had just lost mad weight. I had been 330 pounds at one point, and then I said, *Fuck that.* I lost a lot of weight just eating certain things.

I will tell you the regimen: Every morning I would wake up and drink apple cider vinegar diluted with water. I would have a ginger shot. Then I would work out for at least an hour. Like, an hour of working out—cardio, push-ups, fucking crunches, whatever. Just doing whatever I wanted for an hour, two hours. Stayed in the house every day and just did it, and outta nowhere dropped fifty, sixty pounds over not that long of a period. I did it over the winter every day until the summer when the record came out, and I was ready to go.

But back to the tour bus. It was a huge bus, so we had a downstairs lounge area. We set the blender up in the lounge, the blender and the food processor. One time we used it—never again. We tried to make some sort of shake with some nuts, and we put too many nuts in there, and it broke. That blender was just fucking bad.

And damn fucking Alchemist, my producer, would always buy the Lion bars, which are like a European candy bar with air-popped crisp and toffee inside of chocolate. They're fucking sick, and he'd have Aero bars also. Any chocolate he had, any candy bars he had at all, I stole, and then I would leave the wrapper where he could find it. I would crumble it up and put it behind something else in the lounge so he could find it later. He would try to hide them another place, you know, in a cupboard inside of a box of something else behind another thing. But I know those tricks, my mother used to play those tricks on me. Who would ever look inside a box inside another box behind a thing for a candy bar? Me.

My last tour was actually sponsored by Essentia water, as in I was drinking ten giant Essentia waters a day. They would be on our rider, and I would get a massive amount of them. I'd tuck them away before the shows so no one would take my shit. And then after the show, they go right into the van. It got to the point we literally had no more room for waters, it was that many waters. I am not sure if it worked, but I know I just felt better. Drink a lot of water and you feel great. You pee a lot. You shit good. You just feel better.

I drank the water because I also struggle with soda, with Snapple, with Mexican Cokes, with Fanta floats, with ginger ale. I feel like it's easier to get off desserts than off sweet drinks, because you are always drinking something, drinks are always around. Mostly these days, I'm drinking water—a little cranberry juice, grape juice once in a while, in a spritz with Pellegrino. At that point, I was thinking it's all good as long as you drink a lot of water, as in you could then eat anything. Almost. You're not gonna fucking eat foie gras and KFC Double Downs all day long and drink a lot of water, and then be all good. No, you're gonna die.

So I had cut out soda, and I was drinking a ton of water. But for some reason that maybe gave me the idea that I could just be eating more dessert, and ordering, you know, four different desserts every night. Just tasting each, not eating a full one of any of the four, which I felt was reasonable, right? With all that flushing of my system with the water and no sodas?

But I was having a conflict in my mind every night because I was ordering dessert. You fall into rituals, and it just seemed like I had to order warm cookies every night. After midnight, things are often distasteful, most of the time, for the normal palate. Good decisions are not made after midnight. But if you're up, you should be eating the extra meal. You're not sleeping, you're up extra hours, so you need it, right?

I mean, I'm also staying at places like the Four Seasons in Kansas City, where I can order warm cookies and apple pie and ice cream at 3:00 a.m. In the beginning of my rap career I had to stay in a shitty tiny hotel, of course, but no, not anymore. There's just no way I'm doing it. You know what I mean? Like that's not what I've worked as hard for, to stay in the fucking shithole. Oh my god, I've done those—you drive up and park outside your room door. Those are scary. You don't even want to sit down on the bed, you got to sleep in a plastic bag, like a bum.

So on this tour I would get all the hotel desserts. I would get the warm cookies. They would send them up, sometimes they were just kind of microwaved, and they would get hard really quick. Then I'd just have to leave them in the milk extra long for them to soak. And I like to break cookies up sometimes and just leave them in the milk while I eat other cookies, and then go back for them.

I would always get the pie and ice cream, because I really like warm and cold desserts together. Like a lot. A lot, a lot. I especially love fruit baked with a crust and topped with ice cream. Peach, apple, blueberries. Yeah. Mixed fruits, whatever. Fucking stone fruit. I love little tartettes or crostatas—you know, when they crimp the sides where it's just a little lightly rustic-looking tarted thing. A mixed stone fruit crostata, with ice cream, oof. That's almost just granola and yogurt, right? That's pretty much what it is, so that's why I feel like it's not that bad. There's a lot of sugar and butter, but it's *wholesome*.

With pie and ice cream, though, it's not just a little taste. There's never pie left. Even if the crust sucks. You gotta understand this game: even if the crust sucks, you just have to find something in your mind that's good enough about it, and then you just glom it. I mean, bad crust is bad crust, but how bad is bad? If it's inedible, it's inedible. But if it's mildly edible, it's edible, because . . . you get to put ice cream on it.

They say it takes twenty-one days to kick sugar and ninety days to build a lifestyle. Well, I've fallen off after ninety days. I've definitely done it right for ninety days, then fallen off.

Because then you hit the road. You're eating all kinds of fucking bullshit at all times at different times of night. It's so fucking hard to stay on any type of regimen whatsoever. You're just scavenging, eating whatever the hell is there. And if we're taping a *Fuck, That's Delicious*, we go to restaurants, and nice places want to have me in, and I fall into other old patterns—you know, like fast food late at night, or having people over to my hotel room.

I like to have food brought to the hotel, as you know, I like to create a smorgasbord of situations for us in the hotel room. That's how you turn people on to different new things, just by having an array of things, and I'm not into just one thing, either. I'm never going to just order one thing and eat all of it. I like to order a lot of food. Then I like to pick, to just try everything. I don't like to be just allowed to have only one flavor. Who eats like that? Think about your children; if you put a bunch of things around and allow them to try a lot of different flavors, you know they'll have a more diverse palate, and a more diverse understanding of the world, in my opinion.

Eating can come with depression, it can come with boredom, and it also comes with habit. People are creatures of habit. It's just what the fuck we do. It's nice to have a dessert after dinner. You just shouldn't, even really skinny people, for health reasons. We know that, you know? We don't need to eat dessert, because it's unnecessary. Or is it necessary? It might be necessary for happiness—who's to say what is necessary or not?

So I eat good things, but cheap bullshit also. It's a full spectrum of eating for me, top to bottom. I eat good shit, bad shit, bullshit. I am also addicted to orange Tic Tacs, but who gives a flying fuck about all this stuff? All this is normal—I feel like all these stories about eating this or that are just stories because I am husky. If I weren't fat it wouldn't be news that I roast a chicken or ate one McNugget. I'd just eat.

But I don't get to just go eat. I have to think about what to eat every time. I have to fucking put outfits on, disguises, to go eat my McNugget, my ice cream. C'mon, I am kidding. I use comedic stuff to break the ice with these things . . . 'cause I am a freak. Like midgets or bearded ladies, I'm a freak, right? I'm barbaric. Don't look at him! Throw a blanket on him, throw tar and feathers on him. Throw french fries on him.

And I do like ice cream. I've always loved ice cream, even though growing up, we never had the ice cream I wanted in the fridge. I've been a Häagen-Dazs boy since forever. I like getting a pint of vanilla Häagen-Dazs, and a pint of chocolate, delivered just to have in the house. Breyers has more air, but I do like it. I used to get Dolly Madison, which was like a twenty-five-cent mini-rectangle cardboard carton, a nice yellow French vanilla. But my mother always liked weird-ass flavors—rum raisin—not flavors that would pop off to a young kid. I hate any cakes or desserts soaked in alcohol, that shit is nauseating. Rum cake, the Caribbean version, is sickening to me, like you're eating rubbing alcohol. But even then I would force myself to eat around the fucking rum-soaked raisins and shit.

Really it's not just ice cream that's the struggle for me, it's dessert, it's everything sweet. Like I told my mother, *Don't bring anything sweet to the house when you come for Mother's Day.* And what did she do? She brought the Chinese cake she always gets—it's like mango and cream, and it's fucking fire, and she also brought this box of Japanese cream puffs. I mean, it was Mother's Day. She can have whatever she wants. But I woke up at three in the morning and glommed whatever little parts of it were left.

So you see, it's heavy, my craving for sweet things. Once you pop, you can't stop—that's the truth. Once you put that sugar flavor in your mouth? Then you want it every time you eat: *Oh no, I need the sweet thing.* Now that you've had your meal, you need your dessert. Sometimes you will just pick at the meal to get to the dessert. And then there are times when you just can't eat anymore, but you can always eat dessert. There's a different part of the brain and stomach that calculates cream and sugar. Ice cream especially goes down really smooth, like a fine tequila.

So how about this? I felt like I had made a step in the right direction the other day at lunch. It was a steak house. First, I didn't eat that much. I had one tiny piece of steak, and a quarter of a burger, a little creamed spinach, and that quantified a decent-sized lunch for me. Then they said, *The desserts are on us, you can have whatever you want.* I said, *Not today.* I turned down free desserts. I mean, they have good desserts. I really like their fucking sundae. Ice cream in some sort of tall glass with all kinds of shit on it? That's right up my alley.

I was there with my friends from France, with a natural winemaker from Auvergne, and I think they were good with skipping dessert, because you don't eat dessert after every meal in France. And even here, who the fuck eats dessert with every meal? Do you have breakfast dessert, lunch dessert, and dinner dessert? So I didn't think that it was necessary at that exact moment in the afternoon to try ten desserts.

The night before that steak dinner, we didn't take dessert, either. Then they came out and gave us this big fucking thing with pistachio cream inside, a big almost-donut like thing, a giant cruller. I wouldn't have ordered it. But if it's around, I'm fucking demolishing it. That's the problem.

You can see I am trying to, you know, control myself: Not as many desserts. Not having a dessert at every meal. But people, I don't know, they want to give me all the desserts, all the time.

My boy brought over this fucking Carvel box to watch the Super Bowl. You know the free little round ice cream sandwiches from the corner store that were a staple back in the day? Well, they were free for me—they were right by the door, just asking for it. The store was like, *Yo, take this.* The Carvel ones were similar, little round ones, the Flying Saucers, with soft serve inside two Oreo cookie–like wafers.* But they were slightly smaller than the usual corner store ice cream sandwiches, so I felt that I needed four of them. And I had four, slowly, throughout the day. Then this morning, I finished off the box.

---

* I eat them in several ways: I used to twist it open, and do it that way. Most of the time I don't do that anymore, because I don't want to get the Oreo on my beard. So I also like to soak the Oreo all the way up to the top where I just have a little fingerhold of the cookie, right before it crumbles into my face. So you get like that soggy black cookie, but still somewhat firm frosting, because it's been frozen by the cold milk. And then you still have that extra little crunch of dry cookie at the end. It's a nice little thing.

So yeah, I don't regret it. I just shouldn't have done it, for my own sake—for my health. They say you're supposed to regret things like that, bad things that you've done. I'm not a regretter. Yes, I understand that I shouldn't have done that, but I don't regret it.

Okay, in some cases I do have regrets, so that made everything irrelevant right there. But I don't want it to sound like I have a struggle with ice cream. It makes me sound . . . like I have a drug problem. But I am addicted to what I like. And I like ice cream. I like ice cream a lot.

I am struggling right now, because I have a bunch more ice cream sandwiches in the freezer because a while back I started an ice cream company. I fucked it up. This ice cream in my freezer right now is not for my consumption, it is to give away, to promote the business. I've had plenty of it in there before—I had already finished them, as in gave most of them away. They were gone. I didn't have to think about them anymore. And then my business partner just came over and brought me more.

Now I'm like, *Damn. I don't want to have it.* But I know they're there. But I wouldn't have done that to myself, because I haven't ordered ice cream for myself in a long time. So, I'm going to lie to you. There's no doubt. That's part of the sickness with ice cream. I'm not going to tell you exactly everything, but I will eventually tell you everything.

I wake up at 6:00 a.m., and sometimes the first thing I do is have a little scoop of Häagen-Dazs. You never do that?

I'm sick, I wake up and I need a spike right away. I'll wake up and it's that ice cream, right away. Well, really, as soon as I wake up I go straight to the bathroom, do a little thinking. Sometimes I don't even have to shit, I just sit there. And then for about an hour I'm looking at Twitter, so that's literally the first things I do. But ice cream is often the first thing I eat. It's so cold. It's fun. It's a little weird to have that jarring thing in the morning. I take just one scoop, a little spoonful. Well, what I really do is: I take a little bit of the vanilla and the chocolate mixed on the spoon, but then I cover it. I put it back in the freezer. I'll walk away . . . and then come back and take it out again. The whole pint of ice cream can be gone in an instant, or it can last for days.

A savory casserole thing: I'm also going for that first thing in the morning, too. If it's sitting out on top of the stove, I'm cutting a piece right off the top. Instantly, I'm eating it. One of my favorite things also is fucking waking up in the morning and going and having the leftover holiday shit—you know, all the turkey festival things, like for Thanksgiving or any type of festive day where there's food involved? The leftovers in the fridge—that's my morning-after pill.

My real Achilles' heel is that I like everything. Desserts. Bread. Bagels. I fucking go right to the back door of Syrena Bakery at two in the morning, right when they're making the bread. Whole roasted sweet potatoes. Leftover steak. But the savory casserole thing, it has to be evened off. Always even. That's because we have OCD in the sense that every bite leads to another, because it has to be evened off, for sure. There has to be a neat, clean edge. There's no doubt. I can't leave a pie cut unevenly, either.

And you should see the way I do the fucking ice cream. I don't bite the ice cream. I'm not just taking a regular scoop. I'm scraping around the sides to make a perfect shape, the shape that only I am okay with. I skim, skim, skim the top, until I get to the bottom, because then you're not really eating the ice cream—you're just skimming. You're just having little bits, little tastes every once in a while. It's like the thing that sprays that scent every once in a while in a bathroom, it'll just go *sozztztt*. I want that with ice cream. Just constantly give me the flavor of ice cream in my face.*

Sometimes I'll even do one or two spoonfuls or scrapes, then the ice cream goes directly under the running hot water. You get rid of it instantly. There can't be any remnants of it in the garbage. If it's just melted a little bit, I'll drink the soup. I haven't actually taken it out of the garbage to drink the soup before, but I think I probably would. Desperation calls for desperate measures. But hot water, that ice cream disintegrates into thin air . . .

I know, it's disgusting to waste food. But the only other thing that stops me is to spit a loogie on it, right in the food. On the box of the food, that's easily removed by me. But I wouldn't eat a loogie in the food, that's despicable. I know this sounds sickening, I'm not proud of saying this, but writing books is therapy: I can't lie. I must tell the truth. I must tell the truth on this page.

This is like a diary of a struggling food addict who wants to change his life. Who wants to get out of this life of crime.

---

* I also love the way I look eating ice cream. Sometimes I think I look crazy, when I watch myself eating a sandwich on TV—you know, when you've got to open your mouth too wide and you just look like a fucking monster. But eating ice cream gently? Or soup? I look good eating those things. I also look good eating noodles, I've been told.

I am laughing, but it's not funny, it's sick. But it is funny. When you meet me, I cover this up well. But sometimes you just have to confess to somebody who doesn't really give a fuck, who is not going to judge you, you know?

If there's one thing I know, it is that to change yourself nobody can set the rules for you. Look at losing weight: I've been in the game for thirty-five years, and eating is like any other addiction. You have to get to the point where you are ready. Then you give yourself some boundaries, something to build a plan around. You got to try and set yourself some rules about what to eat that you can follow.

Maybe you gotta say to yourself, *Fuck this, I'm not doing it. Not another day. No more. This summer, I'm gonna* . . . Like my one friend always says to me—and he's been saying this to me for the past fifteen summers, *Yo. This year we're going shirtless. We're going outside, straight shirtless.* Like, I don't care, I'll go shirtless even now, but I know what he means. He means we're going to be shredded this year. This is the year we're going to be shredded. He just said this to me yesterday, when I saw him in person. When he was wearing a full sweatpants outfit and slippers with socks.

So look, I've tried somebody else's rules. Like when I met Diamond Dallas Page. He is a former wrestler who developed a system called DDP Yoga; he has a gym outside Atlanta. You'd maybe call it yoga, but it ain't totally yoga, it's more like using your own muscle tension and doing these moves he created. So he's like sixty-something years old, and he can put his fucking leg behind his head while standing. He's like a fucking pretzel while standing. I don't know if I want to do that, but you know, it's impressive—he's impressive.

He came to be on *Untitled,* my old late-night show, and he was like, *Okay, so boom, this is how you're gonna lose weight: every time you eat something, you write it down and you text it to me.*

If it's bad you put it in all uppercase letters, he said. *If it's good, lowercase.*

So I tried it. My friend Jamie and I were eating at a Buddhist temple in Brooklyn, with the buffet of vegan Indian and soul food. So I texted Diamond Dallas Page in lowercase letters: *vegetables . . . broccoli . . . vegan macaroni and cheese.*

And then I texted them with a question mark: *vegan chocolate cake?* And I might have texted him, *LASAGNA.*

Later on in the day, I texted him, *CHICKEN PARM.* But I think I also texted it to him in lowercase letters: *chicken parm?*

I was on the fence with it, because it was my own chicken parm. I don't know, I think that's fucking healthy. I swear to god to you, if you're on a diet you can eat fucking chicken parm, if it's fried lightly. If it's not deep-fried, if it's pan-fried, it's different. If it's not on a sandwich, and it is shallow-fried in really good olive oil, just a little olive oil, a little bit. So say you eat that chicken parm dinner, you don't deep-fry it or put cheese on it. You can have it with salad on top, like a little fresh tomato and onion thing. And you use really good bread—you know, let it get stale, to make your own bread crumbs. How could that really be bad for you? Well, it might be high in calories, but it's not bad for you. It's wholesome.

So this texting lasted for a day or two: for every single thing, he would always text me back. He would give me a thumbs-up. Or say like, *Okay, just try and cut this out, dah, dah dah, dah . . . You're on the right path.*

That first day I had a lot of vegetables. And I didn't text him every time I had a Coke, 'cause he would have freaked out. Like, *Bro, you gotta go to the doctor, you got to go to the hospital, bro.*

I eventually quit. It's annoying doing that every day, but I guess for some people it would make them change their lifestyle. For some people, maybe that's what you have to do. Whatever keeps you on track. But I never didn't eat anything because I knew I had to text it to him, definitely not. So I stopped.

And then a few days later he texted me, *Are you ghosting me, brother?*

I said, *Nah man, I've just been busy man, you know.*

Okay, bro, he texted. *Hit me when you come up for air.*

Then he goes, *Yo, Bronson.* He texted me a photo. *This is one of my guys. As you can tell by the T-shirt, he's doing my DDP Yoga program. He started at 475 pounds. Today he just got to 200 pounds. He just hit the 200 pounds mark.*

I said, *Yo, I need to get it together, bro.* That's what I sent to him.

He said, *You can do it only if you're ready to change your lifestyle, bro,* with a bang emoji. *Here's an open invitation: when you're seriously ready to make the lifestyle change, you come to Atlanta and spend a few days with me to help you get on the right track.*

That was three years ago. I want to do that. But what I also wanted to do, when he texted me, was go down there to go eat everything in sight.

I do admit that I do feel better when I'm in control of my body, when I got a groove going, activity-wise. That's why they named it that—because it's a groove. I believe in having self-discipline. And I also know that if you want to do something about how you look or feel, really it's up to your noggin, you got to go inside your brain. You gotta be in control of your fucking brain to be in control of your body. Without that you ain't doing shit.

Look at one of my old friends. I mean, he was never chubby growing up, he was always athletic as fuck. But then he got a little heavy. I didn't even realize it because he just looked like him to me, but then he broke up with his fiancée or whatever, and so he went in on his health. Six years later, he's now made a life as a personal trainer. He's shredded out of control. He runs marathons. He's a fucking trainer to NFL players. He's married now, and he just had a brand-new baby, a beautiful baby boy. Saj. He works as a trainer at all the Soho Houses now, he teaches crossfit shit, like you lift weights, you run a little bit. You go down, leg up in the air, fucking flip over. And that's just one: now do fifteen of those. Ridiculous.

My friend Mikey also didn't want to be in his fat suit anymore. He was massive, and he just went and did it, started riding his bike everywhere, not even for exercise always, just to get from here to there. Now he's been like a rail for twenty years. You'd never know he used to be bigger.

I think about Tony Ferguson, the mixed martial artist. He had a horrific knee injury that takes a long time to heal, and he fucking came back a strong and bionic man. Apparently he trained and fixed himself with no help from anyone. Well, I don't know if he had help from some people, but he took his rehab into his own hands, and somehow he did it—he took a thousand kicks to his leg to make sure it worked. He's extreme.

I am applying Tony Ferguson's knee to taking things into your own hands—it just shows you what you can do if you put your mind to it. If you believe in your technique and what you are doing, I think that shit works. When you have a fucking regimen of your own, when you take it into your own hands and find the right thing for you that you can do, it works.

Lately I am addicted to watching mixed martial arts and karate, all types of fighting shit like that, and I am rewatching all the fights of Tony Ferguson because he's a sicko, in a good way. He's up next for the belt, and he's just a gruesome fighter in that his fights are extremely high-paced and exciting. Someone's always getting ripped open in the face, or cut.

So I've been fucking around, doing some jujitsu on the floor by myself. You know? Spinning around. Shirtless, sweaty, thinking about hanging a heavy bag in my studio, getting myself ready to go in. I have been looking in the mirror and spitting. I spit right in the mirror. *Ptweoo.* Then I say to myself, *You fucking piece of shit. You got this.* Constantly talking to myself in the mirror, while I spit.

This is instead of going into the fridge. Instead of going to the fridge, I go into the bathroom, I look in the mirror, and I spit at myself. I've done this kind of thing before. I haven't done this move in a long time, but I am thinking about getting back into this zone. It's a little over the edge, and of course you have to clean the mirror immediately—and you can't let anyone know that you spit in the mirror, it's a little loco.

But sometimes you have to do some crazy shit just to snap yourself out of it, you just got to shock yourself into doing something. You can't just do your regular shit, sometimes you got to go to the next level. You have to start yourself off with whatever your version of flipping tires into the street is, or pretending you're just picking up cars and smashing them. Then you just go out and find your fucking calling.

On my last tour, we all decided that we should be doing some workouts at the gym again and we should walk a little bit—me, Daringer, and Meyhem. The first night, Roc Marciano and all his boys were there, and they're all fit—they all do mad calisthenics and shit like that. They were all about *Yo, let's get this money real quick*—getting money is working out. They would be like, *Let's get down and do some push-ups or do some pull-ups*, and everybody did it. It was probably two in the morning. After the show we went to the gym, and we all did triceps, we did a good workout.

But it's a very brief story, gym on the road. We went one night, and we all got hyped, like, *Hell yeah.* We felt good about ourselves. A lot of looking in the mirror at the remnants of cuts, the remnants of mass. And it was a good time, until you have to go again the next day, and the next.

It wasn't like a big decision to do it or not to do it, or to walk or not walk.

More like, I was painting a lot, which is something I really care about right now. I literally spent all my days on tour painting, right up until I did the show. I didn't care about anything else. Also, because where we were in the middle of the country, it was freezing and it was snowing. What the fuck? I have no business being outside in cold weather when I have concerts to do and vocal performances. What am I thinking? I'm not going out. So I nestled up instead, and I painted.

Today I am mainly working toward being healthier for my family. I'm working toward that. These days I know it ain't just about weight or how much I can lift. It is not about shedding pounds. It's about overall well-being. It's about living a fucking healthy life, period. It's about having an alkaline body that disease can't live in. About putting the right thing in your body or your lungs, if you're going to put anything in your lungs. It's about having a healthy brain, about being happy and mentally healthy. Now my time is spent trying to be a very healthy person, you know? And a successful person, in many ways, in many things.

You can be a little bit of a husk and overall be a very healthy person, there's no doubt about that.

So I don't go to the gym. I do push-ups every day, and I walk every day. I walk the dogs around the track. I wake up at six. I wake up before everyone. I do mad different artworks. Plan a tour. Work on books. All before noon. I'm working. I don't have time and I don't have people that do things for me. I have to rely on me. Which is another thing you should be learning—to rely on yourself. Don't wait for someone else to push you to do something for yourself. You're not going to fucking lose weight for someone else. You're not going to fucking look good for someone else. Look good for yourself. Then you'll attract the right things.

Epiphany #1

Now that I look back, it's pretty far-out shit, how all this happened, how I became who I am now. It's ridiculous. It all started with a dream. No, it really all started with me just being fucking sick of being sick of being, of having to conform. I mean, at one point, my choices in life were either just go be an electrician, or work in some kitchen in Queens or at Home Depot.*

I always go back to breaking my leg so badly about ten years ago as a time of inner clarity. I was bedridden for months, and I'd never had a traumatic injury like that. It was a time of really searching within and trying to find who I really am, the best me. And to do that you usually have to go really far down. You go deep—you reach rock bottom. But then when you come back up, you're hoping in your mind and with any grace from the stars above that you come back up with the air that you need to fucking breathe, you know what I'm saying? Sometimes you have to hit rock bottom to really take that next step forward. And in my case, that's exactly what I had to do.

Listen, I don't want to get *too* serious. Moments of inner clarity come all the time. When you're shitting. When you're in the shower. Any time you're underwater.† But I

---

* At Home Depot it's a simple aptitude test. I took it and I got the job. I didn't ever work there, but the test tells you whether you made it or not, and it said I had the goods. I don't think it would be the worst thing to work there, I think it would be a good thing.

† I am an aquatic man. I like to swim anywhere, in any water, in any ocean. The one time I was scared shitless was in Western Australia, where we were definitely swimming around sharks. We were shooting an episode of *Fuck, That's Delicious* in Perth, where it's just the largest amount of deadly animals that can kill you in one concentrated spot in the ocean, the farthest away from New York you can get. Meyhem and I were in the murky

think when I broke my leg, it was a real awareness that came to me, something almost like a spiritual cleansing. Because I had hit bottom, and I came back up.

I had just turned twenty-six. I had been working as a blue-collar kind of chef for a decade, all over the city, and right then was working in the kitchen at my family's restaurant in Forest Hills, Queens. I slipped. The floor was wet. I was wearing the New Balance 574, which had just a little bit of grip, a fucking $30 shoe. It was very upsetting for my children, they were there. They watched it—they *heard* it. They were upstairs waiting for their food, which I was going to make for them. My mother's friend Madeleine was there, too. They couldn't fucking carry me up the stairs because there was a little spiral staircase to the kitchen, so I had to hop on my one good leg the whole way up. I remember that. And then the drive there was the most painful thing ever.

I had broken my tibia, which was devastating. For the first four days I loathed myself, flat out on my mother's couch in Flushing. I was disgusted with myself, I was angry with my life. I soaked in my own fucking self-hatred, my own self-pity.

And then, after that, I snapped out of it. I stopped feeling sorry for myself. I had a spiritual awakening that came from the fact that I had found my way . . . and that came from the fact that I was told that I wasn't going to be on sick leave for any longer.

---

water with lots of seagrass, diving for razor clams, because you need to eat them right on the beach. Meyhem was shook—he wouldn't go in past his knees. I went under and grabbed his leg. He went crazy. Looking back, I was fucking out of my mind. I don't know why I did it.

You have to understand where I was right then. A couple years earlier I had dropped out of high school, then taken the GED, and then gone to culinary school, and it was the first time I had ever excelled in school. I liked culinary school a lot, because I was doing well, I was excelling, and it was in Manhattan, on Canal Street. I already knew a lot about cooking, and I could help people out, and I was meeting a lot of new people, especially women, and I was working in the city for the first time, which I wanted. My mom found the school for me, but I wanted to go there, I wanted to be in Manhattan. It was good, going downtown every day, taking the E train all the way from one end almost to the other. Every day after school I would walk south down Broadway and check out the sneaker shops right there—this is turn-of-the-century, 1999, 2000, 2001, sneaker shops.

It's good to do that when you're young, to walk around the city and get a feel for who and where and what you are. But just as I was getting ready to complete my last year of culinary school, I was also about to have my first child. So I left school and started working for my family's restaurant, cooking, purchasing, everything, it was just two of us in the kitchen. I worked there for years, but I was a fuckhead, I admit. I would leave the restaurant whenever I wanted, I would come in whenever. I took money to go buy weed or ingredients to make food I wanted to make for myself or whatever. I wasn't taking it seriously, and I wasn't taking things seriously.

My relationship with my father soured, not for the first time—he had split from me and my mother years before that, when I was still in school—and I started working for the

Mets at Citi Field as a chef during the games. I love baseball, so that was sick, working in the ballpark, walking through the tunnel, giving the dudes high fives and shit. Some would occasionally come into the kitchen. I loved all of it. That was a good job—I was seasonal at the time, there just for the games for a few years, working toward full-time, and I was good at it. But I have a temper, and it got the best of me one day when all the heads of the ballpark happened to come into the kitchen, so I was out, fired on the spot.

So I went back to my father's place, and I broke my leg within like a week of being back: January 31, 2011.

When I broke my leg, I was angry at myself, at that moment, you know, for being in a down-and-out situation. A situation where I was living with my mother. I had to work at a shitty job, where I broke my leg on top of it all, so now I couldn't even do that.

You know, it wasn't a shitty job. It wasn't a shitty job at all, though it was maybe shitty pay. I was working hard as a cook, and I was good at it. But you don't make money as a cook. I had two kids. I made lower than minimum wage, 'cause I was getting paid cash. But looking back, working there, that's what made me who I am and gave me a place to be able to work on the food that I wanted to make. I could do anything I wanted at the time: I had free range of the kitchen and all types of equipment. But I for sure took it for granted.

Looking back, I did a lot of shit there and I explored a lot. Sometimes I would even go in there early just to do my thing, you know, cooking, because I was thinking forward. I was like, *This is somehow going to take me somewhere, and I might as well utilize this time that I have now to hone some skills or to work on some shit.* I was literally watching PBS and Ming Tsai and fucking *Yan Can Cook* and Lidia and all these dudes and trying to figure out how I'm gonna make dishes like that, and kick it up. They just inspired me. I mean, I love food, obviously. I love talking about it. I love learning about it. I like watching shows about it. I like thinking about it. My dream had always been to be a fucking really extremely well-known chef. Everyone loved me, they wanted to eat my food, blah blah blah. But I didn't have the work ethic, you know? I just wasn't mature enough to really make it happen. I didn't always capitalize on what I had.

I loved being in the kitchen, but that shit is fucking backbreaking work. And it wasn't my kitchen, I was working for somebody else. I was conforming to Somebody Else's Dream. That's the worst part of a job like that. The harder you work, the more vacations your boss goes on—I saw that in a commercial, a commercial for some shit that was exactly right. I always thought, *That ain't gonna be me,* but for a while, it was.

I'm not going to say I've always been amazing, but like I said before, I've just always felt like I've been in line with the stars. I always thought of myself in a higher light, you know, like I always knew that there was more for me, that I was different, that I was special. I always held myself in that regard. In my head, working at all these restaurants, I just felt like *This is not where you're supposed to be.* But you're the reason you're there. And the reason that I was there was out of desperation, and my own laziness.

So to be so hopeless like I was right after I broke my leg, it's a shitty feeling. It's a fucking really shitty feeling.

Part of it might have even been the drugs I was on—I wasn't smoking weed those first few days, and they had given me Percocet—I don't even take aspirin for pain, usually.

But it was mainly that sometimes you have to get literally fired from one path to start on another one. Or maybe just certain people need fuel to feel a certain way, and that shitty feeling fueled me. My father, he wasn't fucking with me anymore, and I wasn't going to be able to work there, and so I had to figure it out, that's really what it was. And so I did: when my back was put against the wall, I finally responded. It's like when a baseball player tells you the game slows down for them, and they just see things slower and they're able to kind of capitalize on that moment.

Before I broke my leg, I wasn't totally reliant on myself, I wasn't ready to break out of my old patterns, to take full responsibility for my life. I was still kind of cocooned, still young, almost babied, like mama'd, just always being able to fall back on something or somebody—somebody will take care of this, or something will take care of that. After I broke my leg there was nothing to fall back on but myself.

That injury forced me to change my shit, to stop being a baby, and it was the best thing that could have ever happened. I think at that time I became a fucking man—you know, the proverbial man. It's like the ancient ritual where you get your dick cut and you go into the bush and stay there for a month until you heal, and you come out a new person with some amount of wisdom. I came out with a new meaningful life, and a new outlook, a new glow. The glow-up is real when you come out of the bush, and I had just come out of the bush.

So at that moment, life aligned for me, or at least it did in my mind. I stopped wallowing in self-pity, and I started working. I wasn't going to be a famous chef, it looked like, so I just started really working on my music, which had been more like a hobby up until that point. For the whole next year I was just working, working, working on my music, and just for myself. I liked working on raps without anybody around me or with me. Just doing what I wanted, my own thing, no constraints, following my own instincts.

Before I broke my leg I wasn't in that kind of mind frame at all. I didn't feel destined to be a rapper. I never thought it could actually happen, that it could be real. I was mainly about working in the kitchen—that was my shtick, even though I wasn't taking it as seriously as I should have. I started rapping in 2008, when my friend Meyhem Lauren was making an album with J-Love. I was at their sessions, and I wrote a verse for his album as Action Bronson.

At that point, I was already writing graffiti as Action. I just liked the name—because I'm an exciting fellow, you know? And most of the time people can't pronounce your name when you have a very foreign name or a weirder name or a unique name. Ariyan wasn't unique to the area where my family was from in the Balkans—over there it's a normal name, a nice name. It definitely wasn't Seth, it was more like Michelangelo. But how easy is it for a dumb little kid in Queens to fucking change Ariyan to Onion or Oreo? So I called myself Action. Though, when you think about it, everybody in my neighborhood had a ridiculous name. I added Bronson when I started rapping, because Meyhem had two names—he was Meyhem Lauren. I thought that was ridiculous. So I'm gonna be Action Bronson.

Even before I broke my leg, I was already going into the studio and making records. I put out my first mixtape, *Bon Appetit . . . Bitch!!!!!* by myself. There would be times when I asked my mother for money to go to the studio, because I was making shitty money then. She wasn't making lots of money, either, but she'd give me enough to go for two hours, to put my songs and my mixtapes out myself, and I was doing shows. But it was still like, *I'll do it on Saturday. I'll do it on Thursday after five.* I had to do it like that. I remember I did a show right after working at a Mets game.

While I was still in my sickbed, somebody from overseas paid me to do a verse. Then I got about four more of those little gigs—I had $2,000 saved up. I went out and got more work, and it became $10,000, then forty, fifty thousand dollars that I had in my hand. *All right*, I thought, *this is the base for something.* I put out my first album, *Dr. Lecter.*

I started getting noticed for cooking, too. I made it on things like Carson Daly's TV show, and they said I was the chef who quit cooking to become a rapper—I made my Albanian grandmother's peppers and eggs, rapped in the hallway after for less than a verse. This was everything coming together—I was making cooking videos, too. I remember one of my videos made the *Zagat* buzz list. The only reason I know is because my boy Tommy Mas, my producer on *Dr. Lecter*, his father read *Zagat.* His father hit him up. *Yo, your boy's on the Zagat Buzz*—he'd gotten it in his email.

Around then I started doing really crazy live shows, throwing myself in the crowd, jumping. People kept coming back to see me. There were some legendary early shows— the matinee and the night show in London, my first London shows. It was just me, my manager, and Tommy Mas. Then we were in Camden Town, walking around—you know, like we were just chilling. I performed at noon: sold-out, four hundred people in a little box. It was incredible. And then I chilled upstairs for the rest of the time, did the night show. I was living the dream.

My very first live show, though, it was actually Meyhem's, and he just brought me along with him to do a verse. It was at the Hope Lounge, still right there on Hope Street in Williamsburg. I remember everyone got *dressed*. Meyhem likes to wear lots of Polo, really loud Polo. I had a long-ass trench coat, like a cloak—it has elephant-tooth buttons and leather clasps, and it's a beautiful beige-brown-toned alpaca wool. I had the hood fully over my head, my hat pulled all the way down over my eyes, like I couldn't see shit.

I was just chain-smoking weed like you wouldn't believe, all to do fucking one verse. This is my big moment—in front of, like, fucking fifteen people. And it's at, like, a free-style open mic night that Meyhem had found out about. So I was just rocking into the mike. I was mad serious. *Yeah, let's do this.* I thought I was fucking killing it. One verse—that was my appearance. That's most people's first appearance, one verse. You only get one shot.

My guts were going crazy. I was just not even in my own body, like walking on air. And as soon as I came out onstage, I'm like, *Oh shit, it's happening so rapidly*. I felt it. I was all into it. I was so into it that I fucking pulled my hoodie down as hard as I could—I felt like I'd been punched through a fucking concrete wall. And then I had to leave the stage, it was over. One of the homeys told me I'd done a great job, you know: *Good looking.* I just felt like I had arrived. I was like, *I can do this.*

And looking back, I've kind of always been a performer. Me and my cousin would dance at all of the Albanian family parties. I remember us dancing to "Murder She Wrote." I was in a class play when I was really young—I don't think I was double digits yet. I was single-digit living. I did a duet of "Stormy Weather" with a kid named Sarah Wittenburg. I believe we even harmonized, kinda like the way Tony Bennett and Lady Gaga do it. From that day on, any stage fright went away.

I remember another early show with Meyhem, at this place called Sputnik in Brooklyn, right outside the projects—and that was just three people at the bar. They were all over forty or fifty years old, those people at Sputnik—three older black people. But we went up, and we rapped. I was just there to show support and love and he was putting me on again. I still felt like we were doing ill shit—it felt fucking cool, and those three people clapped.

One time when I was still working at Citi Field and I had one of my first shows of my own, it was right outside a subway station in Brooklyn, where there's this big art building right there that's cream-colored and covered with ivy, and on the second floor there's someone's crazy-ass space just filled with mad books like a library, thousands of books, and they put some makeshift stage in there. I think it was all different weird shit and performances, like a massive house-party type thing. I wish I could perform there now. But mad people were there to see me, to scout me and shit. People were rocking, and that was like really the beginning of it all.

I was wearing a fucking striped red shirt and swim trunks. I think I came from the dentist* that day, a fucking root canal.

I did all kinds of shows—at SOB's on the Lower East Side, and some Hot 97 showcase where we had twenty people show up. I ended up going on at two in the morning, but I still killed it. There were like thirty people there, I just had everyone make a circle and then I just rapped in that circle at two in the morning, for like fifteen, twenty minutes. It was fun.

I did all these little shows back then, just like any other artist. In fact, my rap career kind of sparked off because of one show at a shitty dive bar called Rock Star Bar on the Brooklyn waterfront that no longer exists, that is now probably a high-rise apartment building. That night they were having some kind of thing and a bunch of people were performing. And my man, Tommy Mas, he was there with Team Facelift, which was Fat Jew and two other dudes. Fat Jew was like a friend of ours for mad years. Team Facelift, they had these songs back in the day that were like weird techno rap, but they were more like a joke, they did dance moves. They were like LMFAO before they were a thing. Tommy saw me that night, linked with me, and later we made my first album.

All of these things were growing pains, you know, like I think if you want to do music, you have to do shows like that. That's how I built my chops before I could really put anything out. It wasn't actually like some meteoric rise,

---

* A botched root canal, by some dentist that tried to give me Mets tickets as compensation, when I fucking worked there. He didn't anesthetize me, and he drilled the tooth and it was still alive and I fucking went out of control. I passed out. The tooth is great now, it was one of them in the front. You'd never know which, because it was fixed.

where I broke out the second I fucked up my leg, and here I am. It didn't happen that fast. I still feel like I'm trying to fucking make it ten years later.

What I'm saying is, there's no easy button to press and then you have immediate gratification, or else everyone would do it. You have to build up to things. You have to fucking do things throughout your life that stack upon each other. I built this shit through a lot of hard work, and it took me years to will this into being, and then I also had to follow the signs throughout the way in order to get here. At the end there was a code inside me that needed to be unlocked to really make things happen, that would just let me fucking blossom, and that was breaking my leg.

To be honest, even after I broke my leg, it still took time to figure shit out. I had a second moment of inner clarity, another pivot point, as I call it, a couple years later, when I went on Eminem's world tour. I was already working on a food show, doing it myself, doing things that would go on to be my first episodes of *Fuck, That's Delicious*. Being in Africa and Australia—all that shit, all these different experiences, that was crazy because it was the first time I'd been that far outside of the United States. I was up on a high spot in Australia and looking out, after doing mushrooms. And I thought to myself, *What am I wasting my time for?* It was an almost-epiphany: I told myself, *Use your abilities to the fullest, stop fucking around. Be better, and just really unleash yourself in general. I can't let anybody get me down. I got to be the best at whatever it is I am doing.* It was me just giving myself a pep talk, because I had never followed through on anything in my life before this.

Up until that point, nothing could get through my head, I was just doing whatever the fuck I wanted. I dropped out of school. I dropped out of lots of schools—culinary school, high school, high school football camp, fat camp, a secondary school for kids that fuck up a lot, even my GED school; I only went to class one time. It was called Flowers with Care—my teacher told me not to come back till the end. I came back, took the test—I got like a 100 on it, and I GED'd it.

But this—this was something that I was going to follow through and do. I mean music, but also the entertainment world, and everything that comes with it. I don't know what got into me in Australia—it was just the fucking wind. It was the water. It was the mushrooms. Shit got me hyped, and I was just thinking: *Don't fuck up.*

Because I didn't come into the entertainment game young—I'm not like a young, dumb, full of cum type of dude. I came into the game a little bit later, where I had the stories told to me about the people that fucked it up, and I don't want to fuck it up. I don't want to be fucked up. I don't want to lose money. I don't want to ever be down-and-out again or to be desperate. So I just prayed to always be humble. Like Indiana Jones, when he knows to pick the humble cup, which was Jesus's cup, in the movie. And we all know Jesus wasn't a man that was boastful, of course you would drink from the raggedy cup, not the one covered with jewels.

Not like I am tooting my own horn, but in my own mind it's almost like when Superman acts like a regular guy. Maybe I go do some real crazy shit at night at a show or go on tour, but then in the morning I am back making breakfast for Val and listening to sports talk radio—and that's what's important.

I've also been making better decisions since then. That's what you gotta do—just constantly make good decisions for yourself. Your whole life you hear about the gut feeling, everyone knows the saying: go with your gut. Everybody knows that saying, and why? Because it's true. It's not a fake thing, it's a real feeling, this going with your gut, having the fucking balls to trust your instincts about what's right for you, instead of letting somebody else sway you one way or another, you know what I mean? There's no doubt about it, I trust my own instincts now to make good decisions about everything, because what choice do I have?

Eventually you just gotta build up those kinds of attributes over time—and who the fuck knows how to do that without it happening naturally? I don't. That's not what this is; this is definitely not what this is—it's not about me telling you how to do anything. It's just, you know, me instilling the confidence in you that you can do it. It's all about finding your knack. You have to find your knack, and hopefully, once you get that knack, there's no looking back for you, either.

I do think that everybody can have a knack, as long as they have the tools that they need to find it. I think that art is a tool. I think that dance is a tool. I think that all types of organized sports or creative things are tools for making people feel that confidence to pursue that knack. For knowing they can make a thing or do a thing, which is a tool for feeling good about themselves about other things.

Remember what I said in the first chapter about having confidence in yourself, in whatever abilities you do have, whatever they are? Then you get the confidence to do the next thing. I mean, maybe you are good at staying home and playing video games. Or maybe you're good at being the last person to get on a conference call. I mean, that's a skill— that's a sign of strength and confidence, for sure. I take five to ten minutes to join a call, but my lawyer is a superstar—he takes twenty minutes. My lawyer has two people in between me and him listening, to tell him when we're all on. That's the life of a superstar.

Another tool is personalizing your life, taking control of some little detail. Everyone personalizes their sneakers, their fucking jackets, everyone has their own little flair. We can all make our own little worlds. I like to personalize every aspect of my life—that's actually what my entire life is about.

Think about a slice of pizza: Don't just take it the way they give it to you, you have to have it personalized to your liking. I recently had to review a slice of pizza with this dude and we went to Joe's—I thought my slice was great, I gave it a ten, and this guy got tight with me. He's telling me that he gets his pizza however they give it to him, and that's how he judges it. I said, *What, are you fucking kidding me? You don't take control of the crunch?*

My slice had the perfect amount of crisp on the bottom, because I asked them to put it in for a little longer—then I told them when I wanted them to check on it. I didn't let them do it their way, because that leaves room for error. But this guy, he's saying to just take it however they give it to you. I mean, that's not even fair to a corner slice place, if you're reviewing it. I mean, the whole point is personalization—they've got like a thousand jars of toppings for you and you can pick whatever you want. That's the fucking New York City pizza ethic: *Hey, papi, put that back in for a second. Make it crunchy.*

So let that be a lesson: Don't just fucking take life the way they give it to you. You have to have it personalized to your liking. I mean, it'd be weird in certain situations, like sex. There, nobody's ever totally honest. But if you apply it in that, it might open up a whole new fucking spectrum for you. You just need to evaluate every situation—the rule to personalization is, don't be a total dick about it unless it requires you to be a total dick.

Weed can be a tool, too, of course. Or psychedelics, or anything that expands your horizons, not even drugs. But honestly, like, if more people took mushrooms, if they took just a little LSD, I truly actually believe that this fucking world would be different for everybody. I'm dead serious about that. With drugs, you don't think the same that you used to think, and sometimes that's what you need to find your knack.

That's what drew me to weed, to have that altered state of reality. A lot of people smoke weed because they don't want to be in their reality, so they're trying to get themselves as much as they can into another one, and then that just becomes your norm. But it's an enjoyable norm: it's not like a medically induced you're-on-lithium norm.* Weed was

* When I was growing up, I thought lithium was the shit that makes my fucking remote-controlled car go fast for mad long.

actually the catalyst for my life, because when I broke my leg I did so because I was stoned. But I smoke a ton of weed, so my self-discovery is always off the charts.

I mean, weed has been my muse for over twenty years, and it has changed the course of my life so many times. Think about when I was still in high school, I was playing football, I was doing good, I was in shape, but I liked weed so much I decided to give everything else up and go chase my dreams—my dreams of smoking weed every day.

I'm not blaming the weed. My priorities were different back then—weed, graffiti, and rap, not rapping but listening, and wearing nice sneakers every day and just getting dressed. But if I hadn't quit school and gone to culinary school and then gotten high and slipped and broke my leg because I was mad stoned, where would I be now?

The first time I smoked weed, it was of course in the park near my mother's house with my friend Laura and this other kid, Steven. I was around thirteen, and they passed the joint to me. They were already smoking at the time, at the chess table in the park, but I used to always be playing handball while they were at the chess table.

But that day I was with Laura at the table, and so I got a little hit. I was a little pussy and I didn't really even hit it, not really. Before then, I would always see weed at my friend's mother's house: there would be these little roaches, little burnt pieces of paper inside of an ash tray that smelt weird, you know? So sometimes I would light them up. At that time people were smoking these things called beedies, hand-rolled clove cigarettes with some weed in it.

I was always intrigued by smoking, in general. I wasn't even thinking about weed before that point in the park, I was just thinking about cigarettes—growing up, everyone in my house smoked. I used to take cigarette butts off the floor. I used to roll up toilet paper downstairs in the bathroom of my family's restaurant while my grandparents were cleaning the place, and smoke it, because they were all smoking cigarettes. I did that to Bounty paper towels and to tea. But everyone in the park smoked weed, and so I knew that it wasn't cigarettes.

I started smoking weed for real in high school. I had started hanging out with the Smart Crew from Forest Hills, doing graffiti, and one of them was a weed dealer, so we smoked a ridiculous amount of weed at his house. If you hung out with him, you were smoking. So I was spoiled from the beginning—at no point in my life have I ever had to search for weed or go too far—though there were many hard years in between then and now.

Back then I had dealers; now I have handmade pipes and organic growers and hash artisans—though, just like a dealer, they still have to stand behind their products.

Smoking weed was a tool back then for many things—I mean, people like getting high, it just really feels incredible. But I didn't realize how spiritual it was to me until later on. Now smoking it, preparing to smoke it, that is my therapy. Weed is my medicine: I always have my tree with me. If I'm up on a fucking mountaintop, it's going to be me and tree. And I smoke weed wherever I am because it is who I am. I feel like you should always be who you are, why try and hide something? I can't hide anything, that's how I am—I am just myself to the extreme.

Because I love weed. I do. I need it every day. I think I have extreme ADHD and this is the only thing that slows all that down. I can't sit still, I can't stand still, I can't stop shaking my leg. I've been fidgety since grade school. I feel like I need the weed to combat my hyperactivity. That's why it's medicine.

I believe weed puts you on another plane, it is a conduit for happiness, for knowledge-seekers, for understanding and also for release and total relaxation and comfortability. It doesn't matter where you are—when you're stoned, you're in your own world, and sometimes to find your knack, that's where you need to be.

Art also goes hand in hand with smoking weed. I do think art is probably one of the most important tools for finding your knack. They say some people have zero artistic ability, but I believe everyone has something within them. Anybody who thinks they have none at all, it's just because they haven't tried. Maybe start by stealing somebody else's style—that's the first step. Then you make it your own.

I've been painting a ton recently. When I say I'm a painter, I feel regal. I feel special, it feels good, it makes me feel good to say that.

It's pretty crazy. I mean, I didn't know it was in me. How you have to do it, for it to come out of me. To know it was in me, you know what I mean? The biggest problem is to know when to stop—sometimes you just keep going, and you just fuck it up. You come to an artistic decision where you know you're just happy with it. You're okay. And you're ready to move on to the next one.

Art is fucking subjective though: people might look at my paintings and say, *Oh, looks like a three-year-old did it*. They could say, *Oh, this is so shitty*. But that's kind of the whole point, for me at least. For most of us, you want to feel like a kid when you're painting. I don't want to paint like an adult, that's so fucking whack. Like, mad detail getting all the fucking contours of some guy's face. That's not what I want to do. I want to make two people with one foot with a goat, a red one. I want to hit the DMT and then do exactly what I saw right away in my mind.

Maybe finding your knack is like painting. Sometimes you can just stand there for hours trying to figure out what to say. Maybe you just got to go for it, just go up to the paper and go for it without thinking. I mean, that's not advice, not really. It doesn't always work.

Mainly you need to do whatever it is you gotta do to enrich your life when the time comes for you to go for it. Maybe don't be afraid to quit your job. Puffy said don't be afraid to be selfish, in some cases, about your own success, and that's good advice—that's why he's Puff Daddy. You gotta just find what you love to do and do it. That's my number one recommendation—do what you want. Then at least you know that you're doing what you want to do.

And don't wait for someone else to push you to do it. It won't happen. You have to do it yourself.

Oh, and it's never too late, either. You know, I didn't even start to get my shit together until I was twenty-six—and I'd somewhat fucking given up at that point.

Transcendental Breathing

My girlfriend, Val, always asks me to go to these wellness classes with her and I'm always, like, *Yeah, yeah, yeah, we'll go, baby.* I mean, I have been to many of the things with her, but not all of the things. But there was this one class she really wanted me to go to, this transcendental breathing class, so I finally said, *Aiight. Okay, baby, let's go. Let's do this.* I was even, like, hyped.

So we drive over to fucking Brooklyn, to I don't know, Flatbush or some changing neighborhood over in there. It was just me and ten women, and it was a beautiful place. There's no doubt. And everyone was sitting on the floor on an old rug, and the lady running the thing said, *Now go around the room, introduce yourself, and say who you'd like to contact.*

I was like, *Yo, what is this "contact"? I thought this was just about breathing?*

But apparently, at this class, you put yourself into a trance by doing like two breaths in and one out, and then you're supposed to keep doing that until you fucking see some shit. So I was like, *Hi. I'm Ariyan. My background is Balkan and Jew, and I'd like to reach my grandmother. I'd like to contact my grandmother and maybe she could give me an answer as to why I eat so much cake.* Except, I didn't say that last part.

So we laid down, and she starts giving us instructions on how to breathe, gives us a twenty-minute talk about breathing, about getting there. And then everyone starts doing the thing. I'm trying to do it, too, but I just keep opening my eyes because I can't get it, so I'm looking around to see if other people are doing it right, to see how to do it. I mean, I was the newcomer. They all knew how to go get their little mats, and how to lay down. I was over there and everyone else was on the ground, and instead I'm leaning on the ground on one arm like this, like propping myself up, and I was like, *Yeah, I have a knee issue, I have to do it like this.*

And then people started going into their trances.

They were going, *Ahhhhhhhhhh.*

They were breathing really loud, almost screaming: *Heee heehe ughhha ahhh.*

And I was over there trying to breathe, trying to fucking gather my shit, and I was like, *Yo, how am I supposed to do this with people screaming like that, what the fuck?*

Val was in a trance. I was like, *You breathing?* She was like, *Yeah.*

And also, one of Val's friends came in late, and her friend brought her boyfriend, and the boyfriend stepped over me in an annoying way to sit down right as this was happening, and it freaked me out even more, and so I was also furious. I was laying there fucking steaming, and freaked out.

So everyone was already in their trances, and I wasn't even almost there. The teacher came around to me, so I told her, *I'm just trying to get my shit together—I didn't know it'd be like this.*

She was like, *Okay, just breathe to yourself. Try it again.*

And then out of nowhere, this one girl goes, *Ahhhh-hhh uhhh huh!*

She just started screaming—screaming and crying, in a bad way.

I got up. I said to Val, *Listen, this is not for me, baby. I thought this was a transcendental breathing class.*

I mean, they were transcending, they were literally trying to reach somewhere else by hallucinating with their breath, some advanced kundalini type of shit. So I walked the fuck outta there. I had to give them all kinds of excuses, but Val understood. I told her, *You stay.*

I got in the Uber, and just as I got the car she called me to come back, because she didn't want me to go home alone after that. Val had done it before, but she didn't know it was going to be that intense. She said the last time she went it wasn't like that. That shit's not amusing when people are screaming out the demons, all that bad energy in the room. I didn't hear any laughter, any joy. I don't know if they were contacting people or they were just letting horrible things go. Maybe it would be cool to just go into a room and start screaming, but I don't want to be in a room with ten people doing that—ten people screaming and streaming all that bad energy on me. *Get outta here.* After all that, I had to be alone. I had to drop Val off at home, and then I went to my studio to be by myself.

That was just too much for me. I like going to get massages with her, and trying acupuncture and shit like that. Getting pampered together. I like to go to the Asian ladies that do the reflexology and the cupping. I like going to my spiritual adviser, my guy on Canal Street, who talks to me about certain types of stones I should be using in my life: rose quartz, meteorite, and pink tourmaline. All the Eastern medicine stuff. But in the future, I just don't want to do anything in a group.

This is all part of my conscious effort to become a better man. If you had asked me about spirituality when I was growing up, I probably would have laughed. I guess I was what you would call, not agnostic, just someone who doesn't care about anything.

I mean, there's no doubt about it that my mom gave me some spirituality, because she is a free spirit. I just think, you know, with spirituality, too, you gotta find your thing. Whatever drives you, whether it's Buddhism and ohhming or chanting or screaming *Amen* in church. Most of the time it finds you, because most of the time, you know, we're all taught from an early age: you're this, you're that, you're this, you're that. I was always torn, because one-half of my family insisted I was Muslim. And then my mother would always fucking sneak in the weird stuff and the New York Jew shit.

I think you find spirituality when you're a free thinker, when you don't exactly fit into society's ideals, when you're not bound by any rules of society or thoughts about how you're supposed to be, you feel what I'm saying to you? But I don't think spirituality is one specific thing, more like you just find spirituality within yourself. It's all about the search, the search within yourself*—and I've been on that spiritual journey for a while now.

* There's a third eye in almost every character I paint. It's the awareness that we're not the only ones, it's the awareness that there's been so much more before us, and there's so much more to come after us. It's the awareness of things that can't be explained, but somehow you feel like you've known them your whole life. It's like what Yogi Berra used to say: *It's deja vu all over again.* And I understand what he means. Do you ever get that feeling that you've done this before? That you've been there before? I've been in those situations where it hits you. Where does that come from? It comes from past lives. It comes from past experiences—it's like we're all computers that all this fucking data is stored in. Sometimes it's just hard to find that download, like, where the fuck is it? But then you unlock it and, oh there it is, it's been here the whole time. One of my uncles in Albania is a heady, shamen type of man. He believes there's storage in our minds and in our DNA and in our bodies. That download is our genetics.

It's not like I'm going to fucking classes and therapy and shit, I'm just finding my own way of doing things, my own way of getting to my own inner sanctum. I mainly like finding therapy in things that are not therapy. Art therapy is a huge thing, maybe I'm not talking about my feelings, but when I am making music or painting or making collages, I'm releasing something onto paper or another social medium, creating things. It's like cooking, it makes you feel good.

I like doing different stretches, at random times of the day. I like getting a massage. I remember my grandmother would always ask me to rub her feet, and now I get it. I also like my head rubbed, a head massage. It's like an outer body experience. It's like, *Whoa.*

I like taking dark baths. My bathroom has a humongous window, so you can always see the moon. I take a dark, hot, seasoned bath, with aromatics and scents. It's real-deal shit, it makes me feel so fucking good, so relaxed when I come out. It must be scorching hot, so hot I have to fucking get in really gently, and hold my nuts. You can't just jump in, things can be scorched off. So you get in gently, and then you take your hands off your nuts and start, you know, putting the water slightly on you, and then you just lie into the abyss, fucking laid out. And then wait till it cools down, then drain it a little bit, and fill the hot water back up.

And nature—people need that vitamin D, they need the sun to regenerate. We are just like mushrooms and plants, we know we need rejuvenation like they need rain and sun. Why do you think people are blue when it's raining? That's the ancient wisdom. You can't play with nature—you can't fuck with it, it knows more than you. You gotta get the fuck outside and, you know, walk around, breathe out and breathe in this beautiful contaminated air.

Taking a smoke tour is also a spiritual cleansing. That's smoking while driving around, two things that give you that feeling of freedom. Early on, it started because you couldn't smoke the weed at home, so you'd have to get in the car to smoke, but eventually it turned into a joyous thing. Back in the day I did it almost every day, mainly on the highways, where you would never have to stop or get off, like the Belt Parkway, which goes all along the waterfront between Queens and Brooklyn. Taking a nice ride to get your mind right and smoke weed. That shit is about clearing my mind. If I get in a fight with Val, if I need to think—you know, if I need clarity—I ride by water or over a bridge while listening to a favorite song. That shit is therapy. Part of the journey is the ritual of doing it. I switched it up all the time. Sometimes I'll even take dangerous routes knowing there can be fuzz, just to add to the drive.

Weed has really always been a ritual for me, just the ritual changes throughout my life. Growing up, we used to smoke spliffs at night in the laundry room of my mother's apartment building in the wintertime. They stopped the elevator going down after a certain time because people used to get mugged—you could catch it back up, so it was a mad place to smoke. Or rolling huge blunts in The Basement, when it was the hub in my life. Or the time when me and my friends would work all day, and at the end of the day we'd have a nickel bag and look at each other and say, *Nick at night?* And we'd all agree, and go back to my friend's house and smoke on his little balcony in his room, and we'd be cracking up and just enjoying our lives.

I also think just maintaining the ritual of these things is actually like your own religion. When I take a dab today, there's all kinds of different various variables to maintain to complete the ritual. It's not just about the weed. A lot of it is about making something perfect: I'll spend twenty minutes putting this fucking tape on, making sure that each edge is good. Even if it's crooked, it's fine. That's the ritual. And, of course, there's something spiritual about hitting a pipe. It's peaceful, it brings me in tune with the world and handcrafted situations. Those pieces I smoke on were made by somebody's hand, not by a machine. So was the hash, because I know where the shit's coming from.

Today I look to all things like these to keep me grounded, for sure. This is *my* inner sanctum stuff. There was a time I maybe looked to working out, to lifting weights, to doing dips. It's a change, you know, but you should always be constantly, constantly evolving. You're a mushroom: you just keep unveiling layers and layers and layers and layers and layers and layers of things. All of these things inspire me, they all add to my spirituality. I am adding to who I am everywhere I go, every place I see, at any extension of me.

You have to just stack up experiences, to keep finding cool new things and say, *I'm going to take that, that's going to be a little piece of my spirituality.*

I am also learning to remove the negative energy from my being. Not to get too spiritual, but once you start aligning yourself with positive things, I think shit changes for you. When you have that down, the you're-the-victim, always-fucking-angry, hater outlook, you want to hang out with a bunch of other haters, and just be sitting around talking shit about the people who are out there doing things. I'm a doer. I mean, I also like to talk shit. But now the doing comes first, and talking shit is just for fun.

It's like when people get cancer, you want to just cut that part out, right? The part that's causing the grief, that's causing all the fucking problems. So, it's the same with life—if you have a specific person or group of people that are really dragging you down and being quote-unquote cancer, then you gotta get away from that, you gotta cut that away.

I've been told I am a deflector of negative energies of others. I'm a known deflector and aura protector. I'm protective of my aura and a protector of others' auras—when you're with me, bad vibes bounce off me. They don't ever reach you, and that's a powerful feeling. It feels like the weight of the world on your shoulders to move throughout all these different avenues of chaos as a protector. I think I just knock out bad vibes, period.

I have also learned to not put myself in positions where I'm going to be uncomfortable. I am not talking about the not-putting-yourself-out-there kind of uncomfortable, where you should do it even if it makes you uncomfortable. People can have confidence in some things and not other things, that's normal. I'm talking about overextending yourself to do something where you can't keep the promise to do it, or doing something that you really don't want to do because it isn't who you are. And if I can't do what I gotta do, you know, I gotta bail. I've maybe canceled lots of shows, but mostly because my gut is telling me not to do these things. That I need to stay back, not travel, or that it's just not for me.

I also think most of us always have a vulnerable feeling in life, a lasting feeling of vulnerability or of self-doubt.

I think that you just have to get through that—not ignore it. You have to just break down those feelings and then control your emotions. Most of the time I'm able to control my emotions now, and when I do, I'm able to have success. I've chilled myself out.

My main thing is that I also try not to let myself get too up and too down. Something amazing happens, I'm like, *Aight*. Something really shitty happens, I'm like, *We'll fix it*. So you just stay level. If you stay level, I feel like you're able to do more—of course, you have to allow yourself to enjoy everything, but you're not going to go on a fucking month-long party because you fucking did something that's not really that important in the grand scheme of anything. It's nice to celebrate yourself, but it's also good to get the job done. Like I said, I'm a doer now. I'm a worker. I like to get the job done, you know? I'm more like, *Okay, we did this, let's keep going.**

I used to come back from tour and be tired. But this last time I felt great: Active. Energized. Unbelievably strong. I kept on gaining energy as I went from show to show. I could've gone another couple of months—and that's not usually what happens, usually I'm wiped. Things were just going

---

* I never, ever, ever overpartied where I was like, *It's my birthdaaay, I got to get blackout druuuunk*. Never. On a regular day, though, I drank like twenty-four Coronas. A long time ago. I went out on a date with my friend's girl's girl, his girl's sister. And then we did like a little double date, and I drank too much and I got in a cab, threw up a little when I got out. I'm not a fucking drinker. The other time I threw up I was in Lyon, and fucking Clovis showed up with one of the best natural winemakers in the world. We started drinking at eleven o'clock and we drank eighteen bottles of natural wine. That I do drink. And then I had to go perform, so I was fucking throwing up all over the place before I got onstage, threw up like six or seven times all over the dressing room, went out, performed, got off, threw up again, and I was like, *Yo, I'm good to go.*

really smoothly. Things were really running well, because I didn't have any stress.

Even if someone else was being a cocksucker and I hated their guts, I was still happy. That someone's not gonna ruin my life. There's ways to take anger out of your life, and I think that I've been practicing that a lot, but you know, sometimes you get caught up. That's just natural. You can't really stop that: motherfuckers make you angry. I am not saying I always know what to do and how to do it now. I know I'm a miserable fuck sometimes. Everyone has their days. Everyone gets problems. But if I get miserable, I'm not going to be able to make anyone happy, and that's not satisfying to anyone.

Ten Years On

When I met Val, she opened up the light. She's just that type of woman. But Val*—there's certain people in life you're just meant to meet. We had met years and years and years ago, before we got together. She grew up in Queens, too—in Jackson Heights. She's Colombian. We met at the concert I did at the Music Hall of Williamsburg with Flatbush Zombies. They let her onstage, and then maybe two years later, we met again—we were meant to be together.

While she was pregnant this past summer, I canceled a food trip to Spain I was really looking forward to taking, so I could stay with her, and I didn't even mind. Every morning I made her crazy breakfasts, every weekend we would go to the Union Square farmers' market. I was making all the things that she was craving, which was a lot. She would have an *aguapanela*, then a hot tea, then a fucking cheese steak, then fall asleep for mad long. I was making fried rice, crispy rice, regular rice, and I had been going in on my version of the chicken and rice dish that my Albanian grandmother used to make back in the day: Boil a bunch of chicken wings, some vegetables, some aromatics and shit. Then take the chicken wings out, fry them in olive oil, set them aside. Chop some tomatoes, add that and some crushed red pepper, a little sliced garlic, let that go, then put in some paella rice with some paprika, get a nice color

---

* I got Val a ring engraved with *9917*, which are her dog Coco's dates. Little Coquito was born in 1999, and he lived until 2017. That's crazy, right? He was born before Y2K. Also, he lived in different countries, which most *people* don't even do. He's been onstage at a rap show. He's been on TV. He's been idolized in art. Thousands of people cried over his death around the world, people that didn't even know him. He's been to award shows—I took him to the RED benefit, he's in pictures with me on the red carpet.

on there. Then, little by little, start adding the chicken wing cooking broth and let it cook, half-uncovered, so it gets a little *pegao*, or crispy rice, and the whole fucking bottom becomes like a big piece of crunch, but the top is like soft and like unbelievably silky.

When Val finally gave birth, it was eleven-eleven—a good number and also her due date, that's rare. Labor took seventeen hours—after eighteen hours they cut you—so we were on the cusp. But there was no way she wasn't doing it naturally.

Labor was craziness. Val labored the day before in the house, then we went to the hospital, we had a little private room. I was doula-ing, there was a real doula. The fucking ob-gyn had humongously long fingers, there was tangerine juice, and me and the mother-in-law being in the room causing havoc while it was happening. I got fucking stoned in between with some salvy—I rubbed a bunch of THC salve on my head. There was a fucking Peruvian flute playing for seventeen hours straight because the doula wrote that Colombians need native music playing during the process, and so they let us do that. We were just playing all kinds of different flute attunements for seventeen hours straight—and then Val freaked out and she was like, *Can you turn this fucking shit off?*

I put DMX on, and the baby came right out. Val didn't take anything but an epidural. She's a warrior. She hadn't had any sleep, either—she hadn't slept in two days, so she was tired as fuck. Our baby has little blue eyes. He's a really cute fucking baby. Usually they're ugly at first—I've had two already, and I was there for the birth of my boy, my second child, but this one, he was already humanized. He's a little crier, and he's a good sleeper, and he likes to be held. He's beautiful.

I feel like I was made to be a father. I feel like a protector, a nurturer, a fucking healer. I have the fathering gene, you know what I mean? Okay, maybe I'm not a great father, but I'm a decent father. I try my hardest—that's the main thing. I cook for my son. I wake up when I know he needs to be fed. For the first forty-five days, Val couldn't leave the house—it's a Latin American thing—and I always let her sleep the whole night through. A newborn, I know what to do: Change him. Get the boogers out of his nose. Feed him. Make sure he's all good.

A new child is another pivot point. I am at a pivotal point again, one of those points when things start to change. And it's funny, now that I think about it, I am kind of at the same point now I was ten years ago. As in, just doing my own thing, like I was right after I broke my leg. I don't have a record label anymore, so I am putting out everything myself. I don't have a contract with a TV network anymore, so anything I do now, I have to start myself. I am totally on my own again, doing things myself and for myself. It's freedom, but it also means I am kind of back where I am trying to just make it, to stay afloat. But now I am trying to do more than stay afloat: I'm trying to fly. I'm an aging rapper on the verge of greatness.

The more successful I am, to be honest, the less I care about what I can buy. I'm not saying I have all the money in the world, but I can buy a couple of things now, when for a long time, I couldn't. It's crazy, because when I was growing up, no one wanted to give me anything—you know, *You can't do this, You can't eat here, You can't come in here.* Now not only do I have the money to pay for things, to show my love, people want to give me things.

But I kind of don't care about that stuff anymore, it doesn't matter to me. I just look at that as a waste. I think I've come to be more interested in nature. I've come to be more interested in art. I am more interested in creating— and giving back to my family and the people I want to be around. I could just be at my studio and smoke hash all day, paint, make music, write, watch UFC, order food, talk on the phone, and I would be the happiest man alive.

My life now is about creating these different pockets of creativity that I enjoy. I like creating my art, I love making food, reading about food. I love working on books. I love going on the road, making radio shows and working on projects and doing collaborations with ice cream makers or olive oil experts or brewers and winemakers.

I mean, there's another reason why I think I do all these things. I want to leave a legacy for everybody. I want to leave something for everyone. I want to make sure that people are taking care of the people I love, money-wise, when I am gone. There are things that could continue, you know, things I've made or been a part of. I mean, I also like doing what I like to do, but that's also a benefit.

Recently, I just started making movies, too. That's new. I was in *The Irishman*, and that was my first. And I just did one scene, but imagine you first come into the game and your first scene is with De Niro and Scorsese in a modern-day *Goodfellas*? It's something that gives you an adrenaline rush like no other.

It was so surreal to grow up with all these people in my life, and now I'm doing some sort of scene with them. It was fucking weird. And I got to ad lib. Honestly, the *whole thing* was just an ad lib—Scorsese told me to just have fun. It was like me, him, and De Niro huddled together, and De Niro was totally in character, but he broke it after I stumbled over my words one time. I went over to him, I was like, *Yo, my bad, man.*

He was like, *Listen, you really fucked up the scene.*

I start apologizing: *I'm sorry, man.*

He goes, *Oh, I was just fucking with you, kid.*

Fucking De Niro. C'mon, man, I'm about to jump out the window right now. I'm done.

I was recently in *The King of Staten Island*—an Apatow, with Pete Davidson and Marisa Tomei. I acted with Marisa Tomei, which was great, another person I grew up admiring. She plays a nurse, one of those Italian nurses with attitude.

It's amazing, but I can't help feeling it is maybe a waste of time, there's so many other things I need to be doing. The second day on set, I called my manager freaking out, because they had me there thirteen hours straight. They give you a four-hour break, but they didn't tell me how long it was until, you know, halfway through the break. I could've gone back to my studio and done some work, but I ended up sitting around in the goddamn travel trailer, which was sad.

I don't know if I give a fuck about being in the movies, I don't know if it's my thing yet. It's just fun, it's about having a good time. And I gotta say, maybe I wouldn't be me if I didn't do everything. It all completes me. It all makes me feel good.

I think back to when I was in Paris, last summer, just walking around drunk on so many bottles of wine, all over the city. What is it about walking around in another city drunk or high with the people you love? I like that, it feels so free. You don't have to worry about anything. You're not surrounded by your shit, you don't have your regular things you have to do.

I'm breathing in the Parisian air, I'm feeling the life around me. That's a really blissful moment. I'm bombarded with love. I'm just living. I'm free.

It gives me perspective on my existence, my path and all that. *How did we end up here? How did we get to here?*

You think, *Where will I ever feel better than this? Will it just be another blissful moment?* Because damn, I feel good a lot. That blissful feeling, when you've just done something nice, you have a good meal and, you know, you're pretty much bombarded by all the things and people you love. I have that feeling a lot. It's like in the movies, when the guy gets thousands of roses for the room, and the room is just draped in roses. It's that feeling.

I mean, it sucks if you're the one who has to clean it up, but like I said, I'm the one in another land: I have no worries.

Turmoil Turns Me On:

A Postscript

Like everyone else, I am on quarantine right now as I finish this book, on lockdown. I haven't been anywhere but my studio, by myself, and the park and the grocery store, which I do at 7:00 a.m. with the seniors. There's nobody there at that time, but if you wait till 10:00 a.m., it's crazy in there. I am already walking my dogs by six, in the gas mask some company sent me as a joke before this happened. I've been meaning to thank them on Instagram: *Thanks for thinking of me!* But I haven't yet.

I don't wear it all the time—what, are you crazy? My whole thing is, I only put it on outside when I am around other people. Most of the time, even outside, no one is around when I am around, so who am I hiding from? There's nobody out there. But in the elevator or the lobby? Hell yes. I tell you what, nobody in my building even goes into the hallway if they hear a door just barely open. That little click? They back the fuck up. But then again, some people still try to sit down there in the lobby and talk to the doormen. I get tight. Some guy even tried to get in the elevator with me—*What the fuck are you doing?* You know how it's almost closed, and they walk up and stick out their hand in the space and it opens up again just as you were about to go? I don't even want you in the elevator with me in normal times.

I tell you, I even had to make the call about some people in the building where my studio is. They already had to kick out all the people living there, after this happened. It's a commercial building, and it's supposed to be only the people who own all the businesses who can go in now by themselves, to go to work. Someone even made the call on the ones next door, who lived there with their baby. That's just dangerous—me right next door smoking weed all day, and all the spray paint and flammable chemicals from the painting and all the other shit I do in there. It's half of what an apartment costs in Brooklyn, I get it, but the building is shut down right now, you can only go in if you're the business owner. I don't even use the elevator there anymore, I use the stairs—but then I saw some asshole running up and down the stairs, for exercise. People are crazy.

I understand, because I am going crazy also, I am going nuts. It's tough times for everybody, and I know people who have died, who have gotten sick. For me it just means I am home all the time. I can't tour, I can't have a book party or a record party. My whole summer was canceled. All the shows I had booked myself, all the plans, all the flights and buses and people. I have a full album mastered, and now I can't have the parties to promote the album. I can't have producers come by, my friends. That's how you do it, or that's how I do it. You do it with people, you gather.

I want to have a show. I want to be making music, I want to be someplace warm working out. I want to go to the stands at the Queens Night Market. And what about the Colombian parties in the park every summer? People need that shit.

Now I feel like I don't want to be on top of people anymore. Right now, during this shit, for a while I felt like I wanted to move outside of the city for the first time. Think about it, my whole life I've lived in a building with a thousand people in it. Growing up, two whole sides to the building with six floors and six apartments on each floor. Like I said, sometimes there were like twelve people just in my own apartment, when my Albanian relatives started showing up.

I had found eighteen acres about an hour north, same price as, like, two thousand square feet here in the city. I am looking on Long Island, a great spot with three acres just near the bay. I'd just be a commuter—I'd commute to work at my studio in Brooklyn every day.

On my land I could grow blueberries and mushrooms—just throw spores everywhere. I could have a pit. I could have pits all over. If I decided I didn't like that pit, I would just dig another one. I could build a fucking whole wonderful world of all different kinds of vegetables and shit. We could keep bees—I would love that. And most of the time, right now, I am fucking alone anyway.

For a long time I hadn't seen my friends. I hadn't hugged my mother. I went to go bring her groceries—I just saw her from a few feet away. Later it was my oldest child's birthday. Fifteen years old, right? I made her things she wouldn't get in her home, steak and salad and the best potatoes—they will change your life, you boil them in baking-soda water and they come out unbelievably soft on the inside and crispy on the outside—and we ate outside together in Queens, picnic-style.

It's mostly just me hanging out in the studio by myself right now, painting, talking on the phone, making plans. Right now I am surrounded in my studio not by people but by a sea of one-of-a-kind stuffed dolphins I had made that are stuffed but now still need to be sent out and bottles of Splash cologne to go with them that I made myself. This is all for my new album, *Only for Dolphins*. I literally designed the scent, and then I also poured it into the flasks. I filled about a hundred cologne bottles, and it went everywhere.

Early on, I also wasn't sure when this new record could drop, or if the last season of my show was going to air, and then I lost all the money I was going to make over the year touring. I was getting tired of Zoom, of conference calls, of Instagram Live. I was tired of just making plans. All I wanted is to do these things I do and did.

And what else was I gonna do with my time? I am not gonna set up a worthless charity, I am not going to create my own mask. But what am I saying? It's sick to tear that kind of thing down, right? It's a human illness to want to kick somebody when they're down. The mind is a tricky thing—you always have these thoughts, and then some people act on them. You know, sometimes I get on these bitter rants and then I think about it halfway through. I start criticizing shit, and then it's like, *Yo, what am I doing, who am I to be criticizing?*

That's a new skill. That self-awareness. It's now like I have Madden self-awareness speed 100. I learned that line from my oldest son: it's from the Madden NFL game, where you get attributes for your player based on how good you perform on the field. My son says shit like this when we play ball—he'll throw a ball and say my passing is at seventy-five. That's life now, just one big video game.

But then, later on it all fell into place, and I remembered that's just what always happens, not just during this shit. It seems like it's always that you wait and you wait and you wait, and you feel like nothing's happening all at one time, and then, boom, you're back. You just have to remember that while you're waiting: it's always all in your mind.

While this has been going on, I finally have been going in so crazy on my health—I changed my entire life. I started just by doing nonstop push-ups, nonstop jogging in place, jumping rope or just jumping in place. My shoulders would get tired from all the jumping rope. I would get my cardio game on, I blast the music, jump or jog or maybe do Peloton for a half hour, forty-five minutes, but that's boring for me. I have been running for the first time since football camp, when we did the sprints, and the up-downs.

I would just do whatever I could to keep my heart rate up with my own movements, just constantly breaking a sweat. You know, you put your hoodie on, you just put it on and you go at it. You twist it up around your head, then you do whatever you can where you are to just sweat. I do it wherever—my studio, the outdoor area of my house, outside.

I had been watching inspirational videos of people getting ripped to shreds with stuff at the park or their houses—these are hood videos, people showing you the workout regimens that they do on whatever. Pull-ups and dips and shit like that. It might look easy to do a pull-up, but lifting all your body is hard. I don't even know if I could do one pull-up. You don't need to join a fancy gym—remember how, in my early days, I utilized the two metal fucking crash bars stuck in the concrete outside the pay phone as a dip bar right in front of my house? They were so you didn't break the pay phone if you hit it. They were my free workout, right there. Now I am actually going to work out three days a week with a trainer who trains a lot of elite athletes, because I'm gonna get buff. I want to see what I can really look like, I want to unlock the true beast within me, 'cause I am a fucking animal.

I have to say, right now, I kind of want to be a juice-head again, shooting steroids in my ass cheek. But now you can do it right. It is 2020, after all—there are medical breakthroughs with that shit, made by medical profession-als. Obviously I'm not buying my steroids from the street this time around. I want some personalized shit, things that are engineered to get me to my ideal body weight, to make me perfect for what I want to be. They can probably do it as cream by now, but I will inject it if I have to, because I want to be getting buff.

I did have a momentary setback when I pulled my lower back—I wasn't able to work out for about a week. I had been doing lots of explosive movements. Then my back goes out. Apparently my back muscles weren't ready for the explosion movements. Luckily my mother has a doctor that helps her out with her Pilates—she can do planks at seventy-five, that's crazy—so we FaceTimed. It turns out it is the L2 vertebrae, right under the last rib, that goes down to the top of your ass. All the little movements you do without noticing, now I notice. It's, like, all along my back, the nerves are ping-ing. I self-diagnosed myself as having muscle spasms, and my mother's Pilates instructor agreed.

For a few days after I pulled it, I had just been walk-ing tenderly, doing everything slow. After a few days of this, I was feeling all right, then I fell asleep with my head back and I woke up suddenly and I just got fucking stuck. I was squealing, and I couldn't even get a full breath. To have no mobility, to not be able to move? That is humbling. It is scary. And right now I really need to be out there sweating it out. I need to be able to move around, to just maintain what work I have already done.

I got these tennis ball things, like really hard tension balls, to use against my back, and Val is cupping the fuck out of my back. All the crazy redness that sticks around, you could see right away where it was tight, because it stays reddest where you're most tightened up. I've been doing stretches and all this other stuff my mother's Pilates instructor recommends. I am good with the broad movements, it's just all the little tweaks that hit my L2 that bother me. I am still not 100 percent, and I need it to be at 100 percent. I almost want a backeotomy, a back transplant—I want to be part machine.

But no doubt I recovered much better than I would have, had I been doing life like before, because probably just the biggest lifestyle change is actually what I am eating. It's unbelievable, it's just bananas: I've completely changed my diet.

I take a shot of olive oil every day. A shot of turmeric. A shot of ginger. I am *pounding* turmeric and ginger, I am overeating kale. I start with a green juice every morning. I have been juicing like crazy, all the time. I do it with the pulp, usually, but that's the rough way, so much texture. I strained it out once for just the pure juice, and it was luxurious—so creamy.

I've been pounding anti-inflammatories, even garlic, even though, according to Dr. Sebi, the renowned Honduran natural healer, I know the garlic we eat now is technically man-made, as in not an original thing that was here on earth, so that's a no-go. But neither was broccoli, and I eat that, too. What I am really all about is using olive oil, using that as our fat, and avocados and shit like that, and tons of vegetables and good proteins. I have been doing five days no carbs, two days with it.

I am doing all kinds of things, to be honest with you. I have been doing intermittent fasting, not eating till later in the day. I have been not having a full dinner, not eating meat or cheese, not eating late, juicing for dinner. I am not following these no-carb or intermittent-fasting things religiously, but you know what I mean—not too much rice or potatoes, and usually when I do potatoes, I do sweet potatoes. When I make my chicken cutlet, from time to time, I use just a little bread crumb, and that's all my carbs for the day, and I also roast cherry tomatoes for seven hours and put that on top. Phenomenal. I make a tremendous fish with garlic, cilantro, onion, scallion, avocado, red onion, and lemon and lime. I made a *caldito*, a nice little soup, I made fruit leather, beautiful fruit leather.

I haven't had a single pizza in six weeks. (Do I think about it? Every day.) I haven't had a drop of wine.* I have been baking lots of focaccia, just to bake it, but I don't even touch it. I end up having to throw it out, because nobody wants to take food from you right now.

I mean, this is a make-or-break time. People will either come out better or dead—maybe there's a middle ground. But for me, it's better. I do tend to thrive in chaotic situations. When things are good, I can't believe it, I am like a miserable New York Jew—*This can't be right.* You know, turmoil turns me on.

To be honest with you, this change actually all started before the pandemic. I got on a scale, and I was fucking shocked and unbelievably scared. We had the scale because Val bought it to weigh Gigi, one of our two dogs, because if Gigi was over forty pounds, Val couldn't take her home to Colombia, where

---

* Rest assured I am still smoking hash. I am smoking hash more than ever.

she was going to go with baby Benecio when I was on tour this spring. She was going to leave just a few days before all this shit happened, and then they fucked with her at the airport and they wouldn't let her take the dog, so we just said, *Fuck it*, and left. It's good it happened, otherwise she would be there, and I would be here alone.

But when I got on the scale, I saw 363 pounds, and I got scared.* I flipped my wig.

That was a couple weeks before the quarantine, and at first I wasn't going in as crazy. I was still just mainly getting delivery† to the studio, trying to keep it healthy. Eating mainly vegan: Greek vegetable kebabs over pilaf. Vegan fried mushrooms and fried rice. Fucking chicken teriyaki and avocado-cucumber rolls hold motherfuckers down heavy when they're dieting. And the chicken teriyaki is over a bunch of grilled onions. I like to eat a lot of onion, because a Mexican guy once told me that that's natural Viagra, because it's good for blood flow. No wonder my libido has always been in overdrive. But I was still eating mainly restaurant food. And, if I am being honest, I was also getting a lot of vegan cupcakes.

---

* Not too long before this moment, I had to get life insurance, and I had to get a physical. He took my blood pressure and it was *pristine*. I was as shocked as he was.

† The apps, it's almost like Instagram, where you're just always scrolling and scrolling, looking for something good. I'll order one thing, be unsatisfied, then order something else, do it again a few hours later. Back in the day, you could only order Spanish food, Chinese food, pizza, or something from the deli. Oh, and then there was Ali Baba, the fucking gyro spot. And that delivery took fucking an hour and a half, but when it got there, I was like, *Oh shit, we're eating gyros now!* That was the next-level delivery. And you did all of this by calling on the phone. All of those tasted good every time you got them, every single time. Now we can get anything we want from any part of the city, and it's always disappointing.

But after quarantine started, I really just went in on everything. I have been making every single meal for myself. I have been cooking, and cleaning up from the cooking, non-stop, nonstop. I didn't even realize I only had four spoons and three forks before this happened. (I think the spoons came from my mother's house, and the forks were from Val's.) For the first time in my life, I've had food made by my hands every single meal for three months. It's like when you get forced into having to care: now I am really caring about what I am eating and putting into my body. First of all, I like the taste of it, my own cooking, and it is also the most nourishing thing to eat.

And I am not eating cheese, I am not eating red meat—just chicken breasts. I go to get steaks for Val when she wants meat, and I made my daughter one. But I don't even touch it. Not even a nibble.

Not eating meat has actually been a long fade for me. Even six months ago, way before I set foot on that scale, I had decided I was going to stop eating meat, at least mostly. I was already in the process before this happened, of getting off of meat. I was trying to wean off the meat, like I'd been slowly weaned on to it.

I love vegetables and fruits, but you know what my problem was before? I'd make a beautiful fucking tomato dish myself, but then I'd decide to order fucking barbecue to go with it and get pork belly, and then I'd make two sandwiches, the little ones on the Martin's potato rolls, after I had already eaten the tomatoes. Or sometimes I'd just look at the tomatoes, and Val would eat the tomatoes while I ordered the pork belly.

For most of the past couple years, if meat is there and it looks unbelievable? I am ordering it, I am eating it. But I think I've had an overkill of meat, of beef in particular. I am just not excited by a good steak right now. It's just, we've had so many good steaks, steaks that I bought or someone gave me. In general, a steak doesn't really excite me now. Now a more restrained meat situation excites me. A good morsel. A bite—the piece of meat I am eating is more important to me than just having a steak.

A long time ago, it used to just be about the steak, any steak. My mother used to buy a London broil a lot, just getting it from the supermarket, the Key Food across from my house—those are the cheap steaks. And she'd do it in the broiler with an onion on the side—that's why they call it a London broil, because you broil it—and we would eat it right there on the fucking cutting board. She would put the ketchup right on the board and we would eat it just like that. You have to broil it really rare, and then cut it extremely thin. Man, I grew up on that shit, and it tasted good. You have it on white bread later, always with ketchup for schlopping.

The thing is, I think I can eat flesh emotionally. I don't have a problem eating the flesh—any type of flesh that there is—I am that type of human. But I made a decision that I am just going to stop eating so much of it because I love animals and life too much to just eat any meat, any time. I don't think about it enough when I am eating meat, you know? I just think I am eating something delicious, I don't think about the life on the plate. But I need to think about that life on the plate: I would want them to think about me. I wouldn't want to just be an afterthought on their plate.

So now I don't ever need to eat mediocre steak or mediocre meat just because it is there. I am never eating mediocre kebab ever again. I am only going to have that kebab if it is beautiful and the animal had a beautiful life and it was made right before me, or made by me.

You know, you have to respect meat, and a little baby lamb, a little baby pig is such a gorgeous thing. And I have eaten them, I have eaten little baby pigs and little baby lambs. But like I said, I understand the meaning of eating that little baby pig, of eating meat in general. I think I am like a cannibal eating life forces, because they all have a life force. They all have fucking soul and life and a path and a story. You want them to have a good life, to be raised right and taken care of. I think about that. And I guess I think that's how you gain sorrow. You get their sorrow.

I took a class in junior high school about music history, where we always talked about Vietnam War music, and we were breaking down old songs like poetry. It was amazing.* I've now had people do that with my own music—you know, present me with posters of how many times I've done curses, how many times I've mentioned a sports guy, how many times I've mentioned foreign foods. There is always a lot of lamb talk, and *lamb* is not like a word you can use that easily. Lamb is religious, of course, for Muslims especially. Someone made it for us, and landed it here for us, for our survival. The meat of it is also really good, when it's young and has nutrients to give. Lamb has always been known to

---

* Though we later found out that the teacher was a fucking pedophile, with like really young kids.

me for the sacrifice, for us, by us. You're not going to sacrifice a giraffe or a lion: it's a lamb, always. They were given to men and women for survival, for power, like getting-power-on-the-level-bars-in-the-video-game-of-life sense. I feel this way about vegetables, too, about raw fruits.* I think even plants can give us life forces. But now I am just getting heady.

But that's just where I am at right now. And with all this work, I went to 323 from 363 in one month, that's a fucking significant change in just one month. I had lost twenty pounds after the first two weeks, then down fifty, now to fifty-six, now to sixty-nine.

I have more energy, it is easier to breathe. My lungs are not at their peak, yet, but really good. My knees have been feeling incredible. My skin is better. I don't have asthma anymore. I'm not pre-diabetic. My back is better, I am not straining for everything. I can always tell when I am losing weight because I have more torque when I turn to wipe my ass.

It's crazy to have lost so much so quickly, to feel so different so fast. But it's also crazy that I am still a fat fucking piece of shit. It is the truth.

I want to lose fifty pounds, then seventy-five pounds, then a hundred pounds. I want to hit these goals—then keep on hitting the fucking goals, and then finally stay there. That first thirty pounds, getting that is like a mountain that you fully can't imagine getting to the top of. Then you do it, and you just track and track and work and work, and the weight

---

* I'm a known lover of delicious fruit. A fucking ripe mango is good. The sensation they give you is more stimulating than any dessert. And that's nature's doing. Listen, apple pie is really great, but you can't make it taste better than when a mango is at its peak ripeness—they're just gorgeous, they're perfect.

goes down and down, and it becomes this thing where you just keep going. And you gotta go slow, it's not going to happen overnight.

It took me thirty-six years to do this to myself, so it's not going to be undone overnight.

So now I am trying. I really am trying to do this the right way. This time, this has to stay—I have to keep on it. I have to always be able to not lose control. I don't want to go back to where I was when I started writing this book, just not caring, stacking desserts around me, ice cream in the morning, having sodas all the time. That's not the way to live. Maybe if I was skinny I could do that. There are people who can eat fifty chicken nuggets and stay the same size, but with me, my metabolizing machine works better when I feed it the right stuff.

And I always have to teach this to myself. I can't keep going up and down all my life. As I look back over my life, I was this shape and that and this. But I need to stay just one fucking shape. At the end of the day, that is fucking crazy shit. If I keep on like that, up and down, it is not safe. I have to stay in the safe zone. I have to keep my body running. It's really like a machine, the body, you have to keep it oiled, you have to keep the spark plugs clean, you have to make sure all the cylinders are popping at the right time.

The fucked-up thing is, I will always have to think about it. I always have to think about what I am eating, or how much I am working out. I have to think to myself, *I am not going to eat the Chicken McNuggets. I am not going to get ten desserts, and I am not going to eat all the food just because I can.* Even when I have to go on the road, I'll just lie to people who want to feed me, I'll say I can't go out after the show. But really, it won't even be that hard: I can get chicken anywhere; I can get fish, I can get salad and vegetables. The best chefs always take pride in their vegetables. And my TV shows aren't just about eating. My shows have always been about doing things, it's about food and adventure, we attack life from all angles. My original name for my TV show was *Adventure Time with Action Bronson* before it was *Fuck, That's Delicious.*

It's just so much better feeling healthy, and I am getting healthier every day. I'm addicted to this now, and I don't want to let it drop this time. Like I said before, you gotta be the one to tell yourself, *That's it, that's too much.* Now I am telling myself I have to fucking keep at this.

It's both hard and it's not hard, once you get into this groove of eating well and working out. You change your entire infrastructure. You're not craving fucking sodas anymore. And I don't like being lazy—once I get in the groove, I really enjoy working out, and it's a mental stabilizer for me. If I go work out in the morning, nothing will bother me, 'cause I just did two hours of fucking cardio.

You know what else you have to do? You also have to be fucking honest with yourself. When I look back at what I have written, I can see past a lot of the bullshit I was telling you before, about how I don't give a shit. I look in the mirror right now, and I see who I am. I look, and I say to myself, *Who'd you fool this time?*

You know how I told you how I was thinking about looking in the mirror and spitting at myself? I was kidding, kind of. I got the idea from a movie called *Bully* by Harmony Korine. This one guy in it, he hated himself. He would spit in the mirror at himself before he had sex with anyone.

I was literally in the worst shape of my life when I was writing most of this book. Maybe during the process, the writing of this whole thing, it finally made me take heed—*What are you doing with yourself?*

I talk about always being proud of my shape—that's not true. I think that's total bullshit. There was rarely an actual shape, or if there was a shape, it was an unathletic shape. I'll never be long and lean, with a little waist, but you can 100 percent change your shape. I have had cuts before, I have had muscle.

There was a time I could have gone on a different path and been a monster, a big ball of muscle. I remember having a weight bench in my room and a subscription to *Muscular Development*—the best bodybuilding magazine ever, and the only one that talked openly about juice. Me and the homeys, we would all be working out. Those were some of the best workouts ever. I had a futon bed, so we could fold it up and sit down on it and not be a bunch of weird boys sitting on the bed watching somebody work out. I looked up to fucking bodybuilders, to the strong men. I would stay up late and watch *The World's Strongest Man* on ESPN2. I loved how they turned it into a travel show about each country—they'd be in a cave lifting ancient rocks, or pulling wooden carts loaded with local cheese. Maybe that could have been me.

But you know, sometimes you have to go through some shit to get your shit together. It's happened to me before: you have to face your demons. That's what looking in the mirror and spitting is all about.

I'm having so many more thoughts, thinking about more old stories, about being young and what I was feeling, what I am feeling, just going back over it. I am reading the first chapter of this book again. When I say I had a sick confidence, that's just a fucking lie—well, yes and no. I did have confidence then. I had the confidence to always say, *Whassup* to somebody. I had the confidence to play basketball. I wasn't the dude on the sidelines, kicking rocks, looking at the floor.

But I feel like I am trying to come off too cool, and I am not too cool. I mean, I made myself into who I am now. That's me. And I am a connoisseur of life, I do just enjoy life. But I don't want to come off as *I am too cool*, 'cause I am not.

I remember one day in junior high school, I was with this girl and we skipped and went to my house. Apparently she already had experience with these things. We were friends then, and we were friends after that, too. So my grandparents had moved out, and my mother wasn't there, so there we were, in my house, alone.

What did I do? I cooked. It was the first time I had made pasta, with a Dijon mustard sauce kind of something, that I had seen my grandmother do.

It was supposed to be a layup for me, but I didn't close the deal. I didn't have the confidence. I didn't get mouthed. I didn't get fucked. I didn't even ask for it. I made pasta.

And once again, on the senior school trip, all my friends, they were getting head on the bus. I was sitting next to this girl, and I was supposed to get head and I didn't. One friend of mine was getting head from his girl, another friend of mine was getting head. Head was to be had, but I didn't get head. I went to sleep.

Maybe it wasn't meant to be. Maybe it was never meant to happen. Maybe I was practicing patience. But really

I didn't have the confidence. But now I take those times I didn't have confidence with me, too. Now they inform me, they're also who I am.

I wasn't really born a confident beast, is what I am saying. It doesn't just happen like that. Yes, you have to believe in yourself, but you also have to have it installed in you, or instilled in you. For me, it came from my mother, my grandmother. You know, we're all like dogs—we have to be conditioned with love. Maybe you were conditioned with hate—and it is really hard to break that connection. What am I even saying? It must be the hash talking, once again.

I've just been soul-searching a lot, thinking about all this. I just read David Goggins's book, *Can't Hurt Me*. He was a Navy SEAL and now he's a marathoner, he does triathalons. He says he wants to drain his soul of all his potential, and that really struck a chord. I know I have all this in my mind and also in my body. I don't want to leave this world without unlocking my true potential that was instilled in my soul from above.

And right now, with my new son next to me all the time, I have his pure energy around me. I have my older kids, and Val, my mother, my family. All that's another reason why I have to stay healthy. It makes me work that much harder. I don't know if you call that a blessing, me being here all the time, stuck at home, but whatever, we were meant to be together right now. Val was not meant to be in Colombia. I was not meant to be on tour.

I do want this book to be really like something you can connect to, not just some funny stories and shit. But for me, it's not easy to tell somebody how to be. Like I was saying before, you have to find what it is that switches you on and off. It's gotta be a self-run journey. You have to be the one to train your mind, and you have to be available for that to happen. I believe it's always in you, but you have to be the one to unlock it.

And part of me unlocking my true potential is being alive long enough to do it. I need to continuously condition my mind to stay healthy to be able to do everything else. I don't want to fucking die—I am not scared of death, but I like life. It's true, I do like doing what I like to do when I want to do it. But say you just do what you want in life, and deal with the fucking consequences. Other things come into play, other consequences, other factors, like your family. You know, you want to spend lives together, enjoy each other forever. You don't want to cut that shit short over some fucking cake.